3001
THIS
OR
THAT
QUESTIONS

Brimming with creative inspiration, how-to projects, and useful information to enrich your everyday life, Quarto Knows is a favorite destination for those pursuing their interests and passions. Visit our site and dig deeper with our books into your area of interest: Quarto Creates, Quarto Cooks, Quarto Homes, Quarto Lives, Quarto Drives, Quarto Explores, Quarto Gifts, or Quarto Kids.

First published in 2021 by Chartwell Books, an imprint of The Quarto Group,
142 West 36th Street, 4th Floor, New York, NY 10018, USA
T (212) 779-4972 F (212) 779-6058 www.QuartoKnows.com

Chartwell titles are also available at discount for retail, wholesale, promotional, and bulk purchase. For details, contact the Special Sales Manager by email at specialsales@quarto.com or by mail at The Quarto Group, Attn: Special Sales Manager, 100 Cummings Center Suite 265D, Beverly, MA 01915 USA.

10 9 8 7 6 5 4 3 2

ISBN: 978-0-7858-3918-7

Publisher: Rage Kindelsperger
Creative Director: Laura Drew
Managing Editor: Cara Donaldson
Text: Ronni Davis
Cover and Interior Design: B. Middleworth

Printed in China

BE IN A MOVIE OR ON A TV SHOW?

ONLY BE ABLE TO USE PAPER CLIPS OR ONLY BE ABLE TO USE OLD TAPE? • BE TOO HOT OR BE TOO COLD?

MIRRORS OR WINDOWS FOR EYES? • SWIM TO FRANCE OR WALK TO CANADA?

3001 THIS OR THAT QUESTIONS

chartwell
books

WIN A MOVIE AWARD OR A MUSIC AWARD?

1. Listen to one country song per day ←or→ nothing but hip-hop for three weeks?

2. Dress up like a giant mouse ←or→ a giant dog?

3. Wear hot pink ←or→ lime green for a week?

4. Be abducted by aliens ←or→ bitten by a vampire?

5. Go on a perpetual road trip ←or→ take four consecutive flights?

6. Live in a mansion in the middle of the desert ←or→
a shack in a tropical paradise?

7. See ten minutes into the future ←or→ time travel ten years into the past?

8. Be able to control dogs with your mind ←or→ be able to translate their barks?

9. Get a new car every year but it breaks down once a week ←or→
an old beater that never breaks down?

10. Unlimited first-class plane tickets ←or→ unlimited free meals at any restaurant?

11. Dance to every song ←or→ sing to every song?

12. Live in a fancy mansion but never be able to leave ←or→
live in a shack but be able to leave any time you want?

13. Be a happy poor relation ←or→ a miserable stuffy heir?

14. Be a mega famous one hit wonder ←or→ fly under the radar?

15. Be famous and poor ←or→ anonymous and rich?

16. Lose every card game ←or→ lose every video game?

17. Be obscenely wealthy for a year ←or→ poor forever but never have to pay bills?

18. Live in space ←or→ live in the ocean?

19. Eat earthworms ←or→ cockroaches?

20. Only see in black and white ←or→ never hear again?

21. Never have air conditioning ←or→ never have heat?

22. Speak like a duck ←or→ look like a worm?

23. Only eat your favorite food forever ←or→ never have your favorite food ever?

24. Go in public naked once a week ←or→ never go in public again?

25. Say LOL after every sentence ←or→ cry every time you smile?

26. Only bathe ←or→ shower for the rest of your life?

27. Fight with a light saber ←or→ a sword?

28. Climb a mountain ←or→ swim to the bottom of the ocean?

29. Walk with your hands ←or→ type with your toes?

30. Watch only your favorite movie forever ←or→ watch a movie you hate once?

31. Eat dinner for breakfast ←or→ breakfast for dinner?

32. Eat nothing but mushrooms for the rest of your life ←or→ nothing but bananas for the rest of your life?

33. Be made of peanut butter ←or→ grape jelly?

34. Be a pepperoni pizza ←or→ a sausage pizza?

35. Eat 25 pineapple pizzas ←or→ one rattlesnake pizza?

36. Melt like chocolate ←or→ freeze like ice?

37. Eat raw sardines ←or→ cooked alligator?

38. Eat melted ice cream ←or→ cold chili?

39. Eat lobster ←or→ crab?

40. Drink nothing but water for three days ←or→ nothing but soda for three months?

41. Drive a sports car but never go very fast ←or→ drive a sedan and you can go as fast as you want?

42. Live in a mansion in Antarctica ←or→ a shack in a wooded glen?

43. Be a famous actor ←or→ a famous director?

44. Be able to fly ←or→ turn invisible?

45. Be able to control fire ←or→ water?

46. Be able to teleport ←or→ read minds?

47. Read comic books ←or→ biographies?

48. Someone make a doll of you ←or→ paint a portrait of you?

49. Be able to communicate only by barking ←or→ meowing?

50. Be able to swim endlessly under water ←or→ fly to any altitude?

51. Repeat first grade for eternity ←or→ never graduate high school?

52. Live next door to a nightclub ←or→ an amusement park?

53. Have one social media account that you have to post to every day ←or→ seven social media accounts but you can only post to them once a week?

54. Listen to a song you hate on an endless loop ←or→ run endless laps around a one-mile race track?

55. Be flexible ←or→ strong?

56. Go to the Equator during the summer ←or→ the North Pole during the winter?

57. Have a sleepover in space ←or→ in a submarine?

58. Sleep upside down ←or→ swim right side up?

59. Be struck by lightning ←or→ get swept up in a tornado?

60. Never eat pasta for the rest of your life ←or→ only eat spaghetti for the rest of your life?

61. Wear the same color every day ←or→ the same style of shirt every day?

62. Have hands made out of pencils ←or→ toes made out of markers?

63. Have your most embarrassing moments uploaded to the Internet ←or→ have your entire life live streamed all the time?

64. Share a five-star hotel room with someone you hate ←or→ a one-star hotel room with someone you love?

65. Be in a movie ←or→ on a TV show?

66. Celebrate Christmas every day ←or→ never celebrate your birthday?

67. Eat dark chocolate ←or→ milk chocolate?

68. Get chicken pox ←or→ the measles?

69. Win an award for starring in movies ←or→ an award for starring in plays?

70. Drink one glass of hot water ←or→ three glasses of cold water?

71. Never wear your favorite color ←or→ only wear your favorite color?

72. Sleep for only two hours a night ←or→ eat only one meal a day?

73. Have an automated home ←or→ a self-driving car?

74. Robotic arms ←or→ bionic eyes?

75. Talk only in song ←or→ only in whispers?

76. Never sleep again ←or→ never talk again?

77. Give up coffee ←or→ give up soda?

78. Mirrors ←or→ windows for eyes?

79. Smell a bad scent for one hour ←or→ eat a disgusting food for dinner?

80. Ice skates for feet ←or→ tree trunks for legs?

81. Go up ←or→ go down?

82. Swim to France ←or→ walk to Canada?

83. Ride a T-Rex ←or→ fly on a Pterodactyl?

84. Eat bread ←or→ pasta?

85. Eat food with no seasoning ←or→ eat food that will burn your tongue?

86. Never see your family again ←or→ never get married?

87. Be snowed in ←or→ trapped in an elevator?

88. Go to the beach ←or→ go skiing?

89. Find true love ←or→ lifelong wealth?

90. Be single and rich ←or→ married and poor?

91. Watch a movie ←or→ a sunset?

92. Kiss your arch enemy ←or→ kill your best friend?

93. Be rich and ugly ←or→ poor and good looking?

94. Have weird dreams every night ←or→ never dream again?

95. Go to a fancy place that's boring ←or→ a dodgy place that's fun?

96. Ask for help ←or→ figure it out yourself?

97. Ask for directions ←or→ stay lost?

98. Date someone with long hair ←or→ short hair?

99. Have long hair, but it's gray ←or→
short hair, but it's whatever color you want?

100. Send a good night text ←or→ a good morning text?

101. Stay friendly with your ex ←or→ never speak to them again?

102. Never experience love ←or→ always have unrequited love?

103. Marry a doctor but never see them ←or→ an artist but you can spend all the time in the world with them?

104. Have many kids ←or→ just one?

105. Marry a workaholic ←or→ marry a person of leisure?

106. Cry when you're happy ←or→ laugh when you're sad?

107. Go on a date with a character from a cartoon ←or→ a musical?

108. Go on a date with a governor ←or→ a mayor?

109. Watch fireworks ←or→ a concert?

110. Watch only your favorite TV show ←or→ never watch TV again?

111. Be someone else ←or→ just stay you?

112. 15 minutes of fame ←or→ 30 minutes of wealth?

113. Be extra sensitive ←or→ not sensitive at all?

114. Have your partner ←or→ your employer look through all your texts and chats?

115. Be with someone who is afraid to lose you ←or→ someone you are afraid to lose?

116. Live forever and watch all your loved ones die ←or→ die first so you won't have to see anyone die?

117. Live forever but with really bad breath ←or→ live only 70 years but with nice breath?

118. Be with someone who is extra pessimistic ←or→ extra optimistic?

119. Go to church for seven hours for one day ←or→ one hour for seven days?

120. Not be able to taste sweet ←or→ only be able to taste salt?

121. Free coffee ←or→ free movies?

122. Free pizza forever ←or→ free hamburgers forever?

123. Only dance to pop music ←or→ never dance again?

124. Only shop at a store you hate ←or→ never shop again?

125. Sleep on the floor ←or→ suspended on the wall?

126. Have dog food ←or→ cat food with every meal?

127. Clean your ears with a washcloth ←or→ a cotton swab?

128. Learn swords ←or→ lances?

129. Ride a skateboard ←or→ a scooter?

130. Bike everywhere ←or→ only be able to take public transportation?

131. Not know how to ride a bike ←or→ not know how to swim?

132. Read a hardcover ←or→ a paperback?

133. Be a pirate ←or→ a ninja?

134. Be short ←or→ tall?

135. Be world famous magician but none of your magic is real ←or→ a small-town magician, but all of your magic is real?

136. Only be able to write in red ink ←or→ never be able to use pens again?

137. Perpetual summer ←or→ perpetual winter?

138. Only speak in Shakespearean language ←or→ never speak at all?

139. Only speak in tongues ←or→ only speak in Latin?

140. Live in ancient Middle East ←or→ ancient Mexico?

141. Be a Greek god ←or→ a Roman god?

142. Get lost in Atlantis ←or→ the Bermuda Triangle?

143. Use metal tweezers ←or→ plastic tweezers?

144. Repeat 6th grade ←or→ 12th grade?

145. Be 17-years-old forever ←or→ 70-years-old forever?

146. Have messy handwriting that everyone can read ←or→ gorgeous handwriting that no one can read?

147. Write books ←or→ make movies?

148. Play a character you hate in a movie you love ←or→ a character you love in a movie you hate?

149. Start every sentence with "hashtag" ←or→ "LOL"?

150. Go to the beach during a hurricane ←or→ the mountains during a blizzard?

151. Go to the beach in the winter ←or→ a frozen tundra in the summer?

152. Be a queen leading a monarchy ←or→ a president leading a country?

153. Rule a superpower ←or→ a small country?

154. Be a monarch in the modern day ←or→ a monarch in medieval times?

155. Have no teeth but you can eat all the ice cream you want ←or→ have teeth but you can only eat onions?

156. Be an owl ←or→ be a cat?

157. Be a mason jar ←or→ a measuring cup?

158. Be an ashtray in an expensive hotel but everyone smokes in you ←or→ an ashtray in a dumpy bar but no one smokes in you?

159. Be a star ←or→ a planet?

160. Be a character you hate in a book you love ←or→ a character you love in a book you hate?

161. Only ever use a spoon ←or→ a fork?

162. Be a plant ←or→ a rock?

163. Be a bird that can't fly ←or→ a dog that can't walk?

164. Eat like a baby bird every day ←or→ clean yourself like a cat every day?

165. Have a super power that freezes things ←or→ set things on fire?

166. Be able to teleport ←or→ move things with your mind?

167. Be the color orange ←or→ the color blue?

168. Be a snail ←or→ a sea star?

169. Be a vine used by monkeys ←or→ a path used by Venetians?

170. Have perpetual headaches ←or→ sore throats?

171. Have a forehead that's too big ←or→ a butt that's too small?

172. Be in a 90s boyband ←or→ a 80s rock band?

173. Play old video games for free ←or→
new video games, but you have to pay double?

174. Be in a 90s coming of age story ←or→ a 80s horror movie?

175. Be corny ←or→ sweet?

176. Only be able to speak in puns ←or→ never get anyone's jokes?

177. Lose your left hand ←or→ your right hand?

178. Have two toes ←or→ no feet at all?

179. Only be able to use paper clips ←or→ only be able to use old tape?

180. Have everything be plastic ←or→ everything be metal?

181. Be Midas ←or→ Oedipus?

182. Fly too close to the sun ←or→ get trapped in the underworld for six months?

183. Never ever have to sleep again ←or→ always get a perfect eight hours?

184. Never be able to sleep again ←or→ be able to sleep well but always have nightmares?

185. Be a mouse ←or→ a rat?

186. Play Never Have I Ever ←or→ play Truth or Dare?

187. Eat off a toilet ←or→ out of a trashcan?

188. Be a cube ←or→ a pyramid?

189. Always have to wear makeup ←or→ never be able to wear makeup?

190. Live in Victorian England ←or→ in ancient Egypt?

191. Be colorblind ←or→ see everything in shades of pink?

192. Be stuck dancing ←or→ be stuck laughing?

193. Drink soda from your dress shoes ←or→ drink soda from your gym sneakers?

194. Live in Chicago ←or→ New York City?

195. Be unknown in film ←or→ successful on stage?

196. Fight five small chickens ←or→ fight one horse-sized chicken?

197. Have a good sense of smell ←or→ a good sense of taste?

198. Have perfect eyesight ←or→ perfect hearing?

199. Have 200 eyes ←or→ only one eye in the center of your forehead?

200. Be a spider ←or→ a snake?

201. Eat a tarantula ←or→ eat an eel?

202. Live in a mansion with 20 other people ←or→
have a small apartment all to yourself?

203. Be a kid's action figure ←or→ a pawn in chess?

204. Be a teacup ←or→ a teapot?

205. Be a rose with thorns ←or→ a Venus fly trap?

206. Bear a child with Zeus ←or→ marry Aphrodite?

207. Live in eternal darkness ←or→ live in eternal light?

208. Live on Mercury ←or→ live on Neptune?

209. Be too hot ←or→ be too cold?

210. Have tea that's too hot ←or→ coffee that's too cold?

211. Be super tall but can never sit down ←or→
super short but can never stand up?

212. Be a mosquito ←or→ a house fly?

213. Never remember your dreams but know you had them ←or→ have nightmares but always forget them?

214. Be a supervillain ←or→ a superhero?

215. Drink from the ocean ←or→ a pool?

216. Drink sewer water ←or→ eat a maggot?

217. Have an ugly pair of shoes that last forever ←or→ a pretty pair of shoes that last a year?

218. Only use pens ←or→ only use pencils?

219. Be a pig ←or→ a boar?

220. Be a horse ←or→ a mule?

221. Sleep naked in the winter ←or→ sleep under four blankets in the summer?

222. Have an old machine that lasts forever ←or→ a new machine that breaks every week?

223. Be only able to use a blowtorch ←or→ a lighter?

224. Eat pancakes ←or→ waffles?

225. Only eat meat ←or→ vegetables?

226. Always be constipated ←or→ always have diarrhea?

227. Get every new video game on release day but you have to wait a month before you can play it ←or→ wait a month before you can get it, but you can play it right away?

228. Have the memory of an elephant ←or→ the social skills of a bee?

229. Be able to only drink out of mugs ←or→ water bottles?

230. Be loved by one and hated by many ←or→ liked by many and disliked by one?

231. Whiskers ←or→ a snout?

232. Hooves ←or→ paws?

233. Have eight legs ←or→ four arms?

234. Have two left feet ←or→ two right hands?

235. Be a mermaid ←or→ a satyr?

236. Be a world-famous warlock but none of your powers work right ←or→ an unknown warlock but all your spells succeed?

237. Be a witch ←or→ a wizard?

238. Draw the sword from the stone ←or→ be blessed by the Lady in the Lake?

239. Lose all your teeth ←or→ lose all your fingers?

240. Forget how to say your Ls and Rs ←or→ have a really bad spitting problem?

241. Live in 2000 BCE ←or→ 2000 CE?

242. Be 10,000-years-old ←or→ 10-years-old?

243. Eat a rotten carrot ←or→ one of your own toes?

244. Be a ghost ←or→ a werewolf?

245. Watch a sunrise ←or→ a sunset?

246. Break every bone in your body at once ←or→ over the course of a month?

247. Break a toe ←or→ break a tooth?

248. Be a clown ←or→ a mime?

249. Be a lumberjack ←or→ a blacksmith?

250. Be a farmer ←or→ a cowboy?

251. Be an outlaw ←or→ a sheriff?

252. Be trapped in an app video ←or→ an internet video?

253. Be stuck in a newspaper ←or→ stuck on black and white TV?

254. Watch your favorite movie but only in black and white ←or→ a movie you hate, but in full color HD?

255. Only use VHS tapes ←or→ only use DVDs?

256. Have all your music on CDs but you get it legit ←or→ all your music digital but it's pirated?

257. Have everything be silver ←or→ gold?

258. Be a rhino ←or→ a hippo?

259. Be a crocodile ←or→ an alligator?

260. Know the future but no one believes you ←or→ know everything about the past?

261. Have hair that's too long ←or→ no hair at all?

262. Have a beautiful singing voice, but you can only sing a song you hate ←or→ have a terrible voice but you can sing anything?

263. Play perfect guitar but only when you perform a song you hate ←or→ mediocre guitar whenever you perform anything else?

264. Be a master at fishing ←or→ a master at hunting?

265. Be a freshwater fish ←or→ a saltwater fish?

266. Be a bird ←or→ a fish?

267. Be president ←or→ a small-town mayor?

268. Be social media's most hated ←or→ a nobody who people love?

269. Be super buff ←or→ super skinny?

270. Have an extra set of teeth ←or→ an extra set of toes?

271. Be a great white shark ←or→ a hammerhead?

272. Never see daylight ←or→ never see moonlight?

273. Hear the same song over and over ←or→ never hear music again?

274. Only sing your favorite song ←or→ never sing again?

275. Live in a mansion with no heat ←or→ a shack with a radiator?

276. Use only scissors ←or→ only knives?

277. Have a loud laugh ←or→ no laugh?

278. Never use salt ←or→ never use pepper?

279. Have no bathroom door ←or→ no shower curtain?

280. Have no toilet paper ←or→ no soap?

281. Have no plumbing ←or→ no electricity?

282. No toothbrush ←or→ no toothpaste?

283. Fur ←or→ scales?

284. Eat good food that gives you gas ←or→ OK food that doesn't give you gas?

285. Have too much salt ←or→ too much pepper?

286. Read e-books ←or→ listen to audiobooks?

287. Have a pet dinosaur ←or→ a pet alien?

288. Eat oranges ←or→ peaches?

289. Have a time machine ←or→ a spaceship?

290. Distant friends ←or→ close enemies?

291. Only use margarine ←or→ butter?

292. Be the only non-toxic one in a toxic friend group ←or→
be the toxic one in a non-toxic friend group?

293. Friends that are bad influences ←or→ an unloving family?

294. Speak only in riddles ←or→ in rhymes?

295. Have one good friend ←or→ ten acquaintances?

296. Be amazing at one thing ←or→ OK at 10 things?

297. Have a pet tiger ←or→ a pet lion?

298. Eat only salty foods ←or→ sweet foods?

299. Be only left-brained ←or→ right-brained?

300. Have a noisy cat ←or→ a quiet dog?

301. Have a noisy dog ←or→ a quiet cat?

302. Have a kitten forever ←or→ a puppy forever?

303. Put cheese on everything ←or→ sugar on everything?

304. Use only napkins ←or→ paper towels?

305. Have all your favorite foods be off-brand ←or→
all the foods you hate be brand name?

306. Chicken ←or→ beef?

307. Arugula ←or→ kale?

308. Have asthma ←or→ heartburn?

309. Use cream cheese ←or→ sour cream?

310. Be bitten by a spider ←or→ a mosquito?

311. Star in a Rom Com ←or→ a slasher film?

312. Watch a drama ←or→ a comedy?

313. Have free cable but only one channel ←or→
expensive cable but only channels you hate?

314. Wear socks with sandals ←or→ boots with no socks?

315. Type everything ←or→ write everything?

316. Send only email ←or→ snail mail?

317. Always have a staff ←or→ always have a sword?

318. Have great dial-up internet ←or→ terrible WiFi?

319. Be good at math but nothing else ←or→
be good at everything but terrible at math?

320. Have a fun night that you don't remember ←or→
a terrible night you can't forget?

321. Only do cardio ←or→ only lift weights?

322. Play football with no gear ←or→ basketball with a deflated ball?

323. Have bad grammar that no one corrects ←or→
perfect grammar that everyone corrects?

324. Use liquid soap ←or→ shower gel?

325. Eat a lot and never get full ←or→ only eat one bite and get stuffed?

326. Listen to electric guitar ←or→ acoustic guitar?

327. Play the acoustic guitar ←or→ the electric guitar?

328. Say "buggy" ←or→ "cart"?

329. Say "soda" ←or→ "pop"?

330. Say "sofa" ←or→ "couch"?

331. Have a screen that's too big ←or→ a screen that's too small?

332. Watch a K-drama ←or→ a telenovela?

333. Take only bubble baths ←or→ only cold showers?

334. Be a gentleman thief ←or→ a dashing rogue?

335. Have guaranteed perfect luck, but only once a month ←or→ have normal luck all the time?

336. Win the lottery and lose it all in one day ←or→ never win the lottery at all?

337. Keep a journal ←or→ a diary?

338. Use ballpoint pens ←or→ gel pens exclusively?

339. Listen to unlimited free disco ←or→ have to pay to listen to all of your favorite music?

340. Be a dragon ←or→ a unicorn?

341. Always have itchy eyes ←or→ a runny nose?

342. Learn Russian dancing ←or→ Irish dancing?

343. Have free lifetime tickets to your favorite musical ←or→ pay double to every other musical?

344. Be a fox ←or→ a wolf?

345. Mine gold ←or→ silver?

346. Have clap on lights that only work when you smack your butt ←or→ clap on lights that only work when you smack someone's face?

347. Be the tortoise ←or→ the hare?

348. Have to confess your love in a letter ←or→ in a song?

349. Wear something new, something borrowed ←or→ something blue?

350. Kiss a frog ←or→ marry a toad?

351. Have heat vision ←or→ blizzard breath?

352. Have a butler ←or→ a maid?

353. Speak in a British accent ←or→ an Australian accent?

354. Take only one trip to your dream destination ←or→ travel to a lot of OK destinations?

355. Eat yellow snow ←or→ eat mud?

356. Use a map ←or→ a bad GPS?

357. Have your house broken into ←or→ your phone hacked?

358. Have a double life ←or→ be a secret agent that no one knows?

359. Have an alien best friend ←or→ be the alien best friend?

360. Only listen to SKA ←or→ only listen to reggae?

361. Be a boxer ←or→ a wrestler?

362. Run slow ←or→ walk fast?

363. Have all your photos be only digital ←or→ all your photos be only physical?

364. Have everyone be happy, but progress be halted ←or→ progress be exponential, but people still suffer?

365. Race cars ←or→ racehorses?

366. Have a small business that's really successful ←or→ a huge business that's slowly failing?

367. Be a rose ←or→ a tulip?

368. Live in Sweden ←or→ Norway?

369. Be a knight ←or→ a Viking?

370. Work night shifts ←or→ be unemployed?

371. Believe in cooties ←or→ deny the existence of germs?

372. Eat pies ←or→ cake?

373. Have really long legs ←or→ really long arms?

374. Have hairy toes ←or→ hairy knuckles?

375. Have really big hands ←or→ really big feet?

376. Have really long nails ←or→ really long hair?

377. Have really tiny eyes ←or→ a really tiny nose?

378. Have really tiny eyes ←or→ a really big nose?

379. Have really bad nose hair ←or→ really bad armpit hair?

380. Have really loud farts ←or→ really loud burps?

381. Never have the right hairstyle ←or→ never have the right outfit?

382. Exercise your muscles at the gym ←or→ exercise your mind at the library?

383. Spend one week in the woods ←or→ one night on the beach?

384. Wear sneakers to a ball ←or→ heels to a marathon?

385. Ride a bike in the snow ←or→ use skis in the sand?

386. Have stark white ←or→ glowing yellow hair?

387. Wear clothes made out of vegetables ←or→ clothes made out of meat?

388. Be a seagull ←or→ a pelican?

389. Live on the moon ←or→ live on Mars?

390. Live forever in space ←or→ live fifteen years underwater?

391. Only be able to talk like a pirate ←or→ never be able to talk at all?

392. Always have to wear a toga ←or→ always have to wear suspenders?

393. Have unlimited sushi ←or→ unlimited pizza?

394. Go to every concert ←or→ every musical?

395. Go to the concert of your favorite artist but be way at the back ←or→ go see an artist you only sort of like, but you get VIP seats?

396. Eat mac n' cheese ←or→ spaghetti?

397. Eat hamburgers in Italy ←or→ spaghetti in the U.S.?

398. Never get a full night's sleep for a week ←or→ sleep for 48 hours straight?

399. Have one free international trip every year ←or→ fly domestically everywhere for free?

400. Give up reading ←or→ TV for a year?

401. Give up internet ←or→ reading for a year?

402. Give up TV ←or→ internet for a year?

403. Give up restaurants ←or→ internet for a year?

404. Give up pizza ←or→ tacos for a year?

405. Give up sausage ←or→ bacon?

406. Give up tea ←or→ coffee for a year?

407. Give up showers ←or→ washing your hair for a year?

408. Give up haircuts ←or→ manicures for a year?

409. Give up French fries ←or→ tater tots for a year?

410. Give up video games ←or→ books for a year?

411. Give up shopping ←or→ TV for a year?

412. Give up junk food ←or→ desserts?

413. Give up chocolate ←or→ peanut butter?

414. Give up peanut butter ←or→ jelly?

415. Give up music ←or→ reading?

416. Give up going to the gym ←or→ going to the grocery store?

417. Give up your favorite food ←or→ your favorite drink?

418. Lose your favorite stuffed animal ←or→ your favorite blanket?

419. Lose your best friend ←or→ your significant other?

420. Lose all your money ←or→ all your hair?

421. Lose all your hair ←or→ all your teeth?

422. Lose all your money ←or→ all your teeth?

423. Lose all your hair ←or→ all your fingers?

424. Have a face shaped nose ←or→ a nose shaped face?

425. Pee for 20 years ←or→ poop for 50 years?

426. Dance with your worst enemy ←or→ slap your best friend?

427. Have fifty-foot-long hair ←or→ be bald?

428. Eat a million turkeys ←or→ fight a million turkeys?

429. Read a million books ←or→ have a million books dropped on your head?

430. Have a magic refrigerator ←or→ a magic toilet?

431. Have a talking cat ←or→ a talking dog?

432. Speak in run-on sentences ←or→ in incomplete thoughts?

433. Have everything you need with no space ←or→ tons of space with nothing you need?

434. Have foul-smelling sneezes ←or→ foul-smelling breath?

435. Eat fried ←or→ baked chicken?

436. Wear polka dots ←or→ stripes?

437. Drink whole milk ←or→ skim milk?

438. Play checkers ←or→ chess?

439. Kill your enemies with kindness ←or→ outsmart and embarrass them?

440. Get caught in a hurricane ←or→ a tornado?

441. See a horror movie with blood and guts ←or→ an unseen monster?

442. Eat only chocolate ←or→ vanilla things?

443. Have a faucet that dispenses fruit punch ←or→ soda?

444. Fart when you walk ←or→ burp when you run?

445. Get up at 6am every day ←or→ stay up until 2am every night?

446. Have a stuffy nose ←or→ a sore throat?

447. Sleep with an overstuffed pillow ←or→ with a flat pillow?

448. Ride a scooter ←or→ a bike?

449. Roller skate ←or→ rollerblade?

450. Only be able to dance to disco ←or→ have no rhythm at all?

451. Use a wide-ruled notebook ←or→ a narrow-ruled composition book?

452. Only be able to drink sodas forever ←or→
never be able to drink soda again?

453. Have free WiFi but bad cell service ←or→ great cell service but
expensive WiFi?

454. Have a free phone that can only get one app ←or→
an expensive phone that can get all apps?

455. Never wash dishes again ←or→ never clean a toilet again?

456. Never have to mop again ←or→ never do laundry again?

457. Never run out of phone battery ←or→ never run out of data?

458. Have unlimited phone battery ←or→ have unlimited WiFi no matter where you are?

459. Have your dream job ←or→ live in your dream house?

460. Have an infected tattoo ←or→ an infected piercing?

461. Be very sick for one year ←or→ in severe pain for one day?

462. Get a million dollars every morning that you have to spend by midnight ←or→ get a thousand dollars a week that you can spend whenever you'd like?

463. Be misunderstood by humans but understood by dogs ←or→ misunderstood by dogs but understood by humans?

464. Be kept awake by a barking dog for an entire week ←or→ by a meowing cat for an entire year?

465. Wear one color each day ←or→ seven colors every day?

466. Have an all-expenses paid dream vacation ←or→ $50K to do with whatever you want?

467. Have free lifetime tickets to your favorite theme park ←or→ free lifetime meals at your favorite restaurant?

468. Have super sensitive taste ←or→ super sensitive smell?

469. Perform as a circus clown ←or→ a lion tamer?

470. Never lose your keys ←or→ never lose your phone?

471. Lose all your memories ←or→ all your money?

472. Live without hot water ←or→ air conditioning?

473. Know when you're going to die ←or→ how you're going to die?

474. Give up social media ←or→ give up TV?

475. Be chased by police ←or→ a clown?

476. Live with a spider ←or→ a scorpion?

477. Live in a spider-infested mansion ←or→ a pest-free trailer?

478. Get drunk from one sip of alcohol ←or→ never get drunk no matter how much you drink?

479. Lose all of your possessions ←or→ lose all of your organs?

480. Lie to get your dream job ←or→ be honest but work a job you hate?

481. Be rich but hurting people ←or→ poor but helping people?

482. Be alone and happy ←or→ married and miserable?

483. Be married and happy ←or→ alone and miserable?

484. Be rich and miserable ←or→ poor and happy?

485. Be married and unattractive ←or→ single and gorgeous?

486. Lose all your memories but be able to make new ones ←or→ never make new memories and keep all your old ones?

487. Be famous now but forgotten after you die ←or→ be unknown now and famous after you die?

488. Be reincarnated with the knowledge you have now ←or→ start all over with a new life?

489. Fly first class free on a single one-hour flight ←or→ have free tickets to fly basic economy for life?

490. Win every card game but have no friends ←or→ lose every card game but be super popular?

491. Have your jeans be two sizes too small ←or→ two sizes too big?

492. Have your shoes be two sizes too small ←or→ two sizes too big?

493. Have your underwear be two sizes too small ←or→ two sizes too big?

494. Eat a spoonful of hot sauce ←or→ a spoonful of wasabi?

495. Eat a chocolate covered ant ←or→ a salted beetle?

496. Eat rattlesnakes ←or→ alligators?

497. Live in a mansion with see-through walls ←or→ a shack with privacy?

498. Wake up in a new person's body every Friday for the rest of your life ←or→ live in only one person's body for one year?

499. Have a twin who gets blamed for everything bad you do ←or→ a twin who does bad stuff that you get blamed for?

500. Play kickball ←or→ dodgeball?

501. Swing ←or→ go down a slide?

502. Be able to go across monkey bars ←or→ do 20 pull-ups?

503. Be able to lift 200 lbs. without a spotter ←or→ 500 lbs. with a spotter?

504. Eat melted ice cream ←or→ frozen soup?

505. Be a gold medalist but never play sports again ←or→ play sports all your life but never win a big medal?

506. Never eat cheese again ←or→ never eat chocolate again?

507. Never eat pancakes again ←or→ never eat waffles again?

508. Eat all the frozen yogurt you want ←or→ never have ice cream again?

509. Only take showers in the winter ←or→ only take baths in the summer?

510. Give up WiFi ←or→ books?

511. Give up video games ←or→ movies?

512. Get $4,000 once a month ←or→ $1,000 once a week?

513. Die young with no regrets ←or→ die older with a lot of regrets?

514. Feel young and look old ←or→ look young and feel old?

515. Text only in emojis ←or→ take all calls only via video chat?

516. Get $50 million once ←or→ $10 million five times?

517. Be rich ←or→ smart?

518. Be funny ←or→ smart?

519. Be attractive ←or→ smart?

520. Swim fast ←or→ run fast?

521. Give up potato chips ←or→ French fries?

522. Give up hamburgers ←or→ hot dogs?

523. Eat fried pickles ←or→ fried zucchini?

524. Eat 100 chicken nuggets ←or→ one cricket?

525. Have giant ears and a small nose ←or→ a big nose and little ears?

526. Only watch the news ←or→ cartoons?

527. Smell burned popcorn ←or→ burned bacon?

528. Have to pee with no bathroom in sight ←or→
be hungry with no food in sight?

529. Be a tornado ←or→ a hurricane?

530. Be a snowflake ←or→ a raindrop?

531. Be caught in a blizzard ←or→ a typhoon?

532. Have a pet tiger ←or→ a pet panda?

533. Dance with a grizzly bear ←or→ hippo?

534. Have a great date you don't remember ←or→
a terrible date you can't forget?

535. Never see your best friend ←or→ never see your favorite family member?

536. Keep printed pictures forever ←or→ lose all your digital pictures?

537. Compete in the summer Olympics ←or→ winter Olympics?

538. Be a figure skater ←or→ a gymnast?

539. Be an awesome gymnast ←or→ a terrible figure skater?

540. Be an awesome figure skater ←or→ a terrible gymnast?

541. Spend the day in dry heat ←or→ humid heat?

542. Vacation in the mountains ←or→ on a tropical island?

543. Turn in perfect work late ←or→ turn in sloppy work early?

544. Be a queen for a day ←or→ a princess for a year?

545. Be a king for a day ←or→ a prince for a year?

546. Own a lot of land but struggle with bills ←or→ own no land but never have bills?

547. Eat a pretzel dipped in chocolate ←or→ one dipped in cheese?

548. Watch one ballet ←or→ five musicals?

549. Be a world famous dancer ←or→ a world famous actor?

550. Have a popular video channel but everyone forgets your videos once they've seen them ←or→ a small video channel where people remember all your content?

551. Sit on a pizza ←or→ sleep on a sandwich?

552. Sit on a sandwich ←or→ sleep on a pizza?

553. Have your dream job but you work 80 hours a week ←or→ a job you hate but you only work 20 hours a week?

554. Have your favorite food and be hungry after ←or→ have a meal you hate but be full after?

555. Eat your favorite food every day for a year ←or→ a food you hate for every meal in one day?

556. Hug your favorite celebrity but never remember ←or→ hang out with a celebrity you hate?

557. Meet your favorite celebrity ←or→ be your favorite celebrity?

558. Shoot a movie on location ←or→ on a film set?

559. Work for 20 seasons on the same TV show ←or→ work for one season on 20 different shows?

560. Work for five seasons on a show you hate ←or→ one season on a show you love?

561. Have an unlimited supply of ice cream you feel "meh" about ←or→ have to pay double for your favorite ice cream?

562. Have a street ←or→ a town named after you?

563. Win a movie award ←or→ a music award?

564. Present at an awards show ←or→ win an award?

565. Party with celebrities but you're not allowed in the VIP section ←or→ party with your friends but you're the main VIP?

566. Interview celebrities on the red carpet ←or→ be interviewed on the red carpet?

567. Wear a free designer outfit that you hate ←or→ an expensive off-rack outfit that you love?

568. Speak only in hip-hop rhymes ←or→ sing only with country music twang?

569. Go 100 years into the future ←or→ 100 years into the past?

570. Be able to survive in outer space ←or→ inside a volcano?

571. Spend the day in Paris ←or→ in Rome?

572. Climb the Eifel Tower ←or→ the Washington Monument?

573. Be stuck on a road trip for six hours ←or→ stuck on a cruise ship for six years?

574. Be allergic to dogs ←or→ cats?

575. Adopt a mutt ←or→ buy a purebred?

576. Watch a parade ←or→ march in a parade?

577. Be on a game show but lose ←or→ be in the audience of a game show and get a gift for attending?

578. Get $100 guaranteed ←or→ risk it for $1000, but there is only a 20% chance of winning?

579. Lick your plate in public ←or→ break a plate in private?

580. Fall every time you go out ←or→ stay home and never fall?

581. Fall every time you go out but never break a bone ←or→ never fall but break bones every day?

582. Read the book ←or→ watch the movie?

583. Have skin made of glass ←or→ a glass made of skin?

584. Eat only soggy cereal ←or→ only eat crunchy cake?

585. Be able to climb anywhere, but always need help getting down ←or→ be able to walk anywhere, but always need a ride home?

586. Ride a bike uphill ←or→ a skateboard downhill?

587. Regular bicycle ←or→ motorcycle?

588. Never pay for books ←or→ never pay for movies?

589. Never pay for seafood ←or→ never pay for steak?

590. Plan a big wedding that only five people attend ←or→ a small wedding that 100 people attend?

591. Have strong legs ←or→ strong arms?

592. Never get tired ←or→ never get hungry?

593. Never gain weight ←or→ never grow tall?

594. Hang glide ←or→ skydive?

595. Bowl a perfect game once ←or→ a consistent game always?

596. Have one bee sting ←or→ 25 mosquito bites?

597. Be a great painter ←or→ a great photographer?

598. Have one art piece in a museum ←or→ 25 art pieces in a gallery?

599. Have an ugly, priceless jewel ←or→ a beautiful cheap jewel?

600. Have a jet pack ←or→ a private jet?

601. Have a private movie theatre ←or→ a private arcade?

602. Have a heated pool ←or→ a hot tub?

603. Run 26 miles in one day ←or→ one mile every day for 26 days?

604. Run 5K in one day ←or→ 1K every day for 5 days?

605. Live next to a stinky factory ←or→ next to the city dump?

606. Eat scrambled eggs with jelly ←or→ toast with ketchup?

607. Eat fried chicken with mustard ←or→ a hot dog with mayonnaise?

608. Cuddle with snakes ←or→ cuddle with worms?

609. Have one ten-dollar bill ←or→ ten one-dollar bills?

610. Learn by osmosis ←or→ get full by osmosis?

611. Fly a fighter jet ←or→ a helicopter?

612. Surf ←or→ snowboard?

613. Sleep in the snow ←or→ run in the sand?

614. Eat meat with sugar ←or→ cake with salt?

615. Discover a new star ←or→ a new planet?

616. Discover a new color ←or→ a new sound?

617. Discover a new language ←or→ a new dance?

618. Own a fancy microscope ←or→ a fancy telescope?

619. Be a scientist ←or→ an astronaut?

620. Be able to change your appearance at will ←or→ hold your breath forever?

621. Drink juice with no sugar ←or→ soda with no fizz?

622. Own a quiet, small restaurant that serves great food ←or→ a huge, famous restaurant that serves bad food?

623. Ride a roller coaster ←or→ a merry-go-round?

624. Party all day ←or→ party all night?

625. Ski in the Alps ←or→ vacation in the Caribbean?

626. Play in a giant mud puddle ←or→ a giant sandbox?

627. Spend the day on a yacht ←or→ go on an all-expenses paid shopping spree?

628. Camp in a luxurious tent ←or→ sleep in a grungy hotel room?

629. Hear your favorite song played on a loop for 24 hours ←or→ song you hate played once a day for 24 days?

630. Take a vow of silence ←or→ a vow of celibacy?

631. Work in an office ←or→ work outside?

632. Work as a CEO for a low salary ←or→ do manual labor for a high salary?

633. Work in a cubicle that's quiet ←or→ an office that's loud?

634. Pack your lunch ←or→ buy your lunch?

635. Live forever with an eyelash in your eye ←or→ a cat hair in your throat?

636. Live forever with a lump in your throat ←or→ a lump on your forehead?

637. Have eyebrows that never stop growing ←or→ a nose that never stops growing?

638. Have tiny ears ←or→ a tiny mouth?

639. Have a tiny mouth ←or→ big ears?

640. Have a big mouth ←or→ tiny ears?

641. Pierce your nose ←or→ your eyebrow?

642. Pierce your belly button ←or→ your ear?

643. Only whisper ←or→ yell?

644. Have a tiny nose but big hands ←or→ tiny hands but a big nose?

645. Get a tattoo of your face ←or→ a tattoo on your face?

646. Bite your tongue ←or→ get a paper cut?

647. Stub your toe ←or→ bite your tongue?

648. Pee every time you laugh ←or→ fart every time you cry?

649. Only communicate by video chat ←or→ message boards?

650. Sweat lemonade ←or→ bleed raspberry jam?

651. Be allergic to sunlight ←or→ allergic to water?

652. Date someone older than you ←or→ younger than you?

653. Date someone taller than you ←or→ shorter than you?

654. Date someone smarter than you ←or→ someone dumber than you?

655. Date someone who was better than you at everything ←or→ worse than you at everything?

656. Be lucky for only one hour every day ←or→ one whole day every month?

657. Find $5 every day for the rest of your life ←or→ find $1000 every month for a year?

658. Go on a blind date ←or→ use a dating service?

659. Have an arranged marriage ←or→ marry someone you hate?

660. Ride an elephant ←or→ a camel?

661. Climb a tree ←or→ climb monkey bars?

662. Get cheated on and never know ←or→ never get cheated on but always worry?

663. Have an unfriendly cat ←or→ a friendly dog?

664. Have a mean dog ←or→ friendly cat?

665. Have to get a new goldfish every day ←or→ one gold fish that lives forever?

666. Spend a day in Tokyo ←or→ a night in Venice?

667. Never sit on the floor ←or→ never sit on a chair?

668. Have ears for thumbs ←or→ eyes for fingers?

669. Remember everything you see ←or→ record everything you hear?

670. Have a photographic memory ←or→ be able to read minds?

671. Know what everyone is thinking of you but never be able to say what you think of them ←or→ only be able to tell them what you think of them?

672. Change the TV channel with your mind ←or→ turn lights on and off with your mind?

673. Listen to talk radio for an hour every day ←or→ a country station for 24 hours straight?

674. Eat candy for breakfast ←or→ bacon for dessert?

675. Mix pasta with syrup ←or→ mix garlic with pancakes?

676. Sit on a tack ←or→ step on a nail?

677. Sit on a nail ←or→ step on a tack?

678. Break one valuable thing ←or→ many things you just like a lot?

679. Break your knee but keep your job ←or→ stay whole but never be able to find work again?

680. Smell like baby powder ←or→ baby lotion?

681. Switch your eyes and ears ←or→ your nose and mouth?

682. Suck your toe ←or→ stub your thumb?

683. Fly a kite ←or→ hang glide?

684. Climb a mountain ←or→ traverse a dessert?

685. Get something new every day for a year ←or→
big and expensive thing every year for ten years?

686. Take a cruise around the world ←or→ fly around the world?

687. See a comet ←or→ see a meteor?

688. Meet an alien ←or→ a vampire?

689. Meet a werewolf ←or→ a ghost?

690. Be turned into a vampire ←or→ bitten by a werewolf?

691. Be drowned by a siren ←or→ abducted by an alien?

692. Give up your voice to be with the one you love ←or→ give up the one you love to keep your voice?

693. Wish on a star ←or→ wish on a birthday cake?

694. Ride in a rocket ←or→ ride in a submarine?

695. Own a yacht ←or→ own a private jet?

696. Be able to see in the dark ←or→ hear underwater?

697. Live on a deserted island ←or→ in a crowded city?

698. Live as a rancher ←or→ a farmer?

699. Raise cows ←or→ sheep?

700. Raise chickens ←or→ turkeys?

701. Drink chocolate milk ←or→ strawberry milk?

702. Eat cheese but it makes you fart ←or→ never eat cheese at all?

703. Be covered in slime ←or→ covered in sugar?

704. Have a glamorous party in a small town ←or→ a simple party in a big city?

705. Fly in a subpar private jet ←or→ first class on a commercial airline?

706. Fly first class but sit next to someone who smells bad ←or→ economy where the air is much fresher?

707. Fly first class but get no free meal ←or→ economy and get a gourmet dish?

708. Break your mother's favorite china ←or→ lose your favorite shirt?

709. Sleep with the TV on ←or→ sleep with the radio on?

710. Listen to your favorite song ←or→ watch your favorite TV show?

711. Read your favorite book ←or→ watch your favorite movie?

712. Meet your favorite actor ←or→ meet your favorite singer?

713. Act in a movie with your favorite actor ←or→ write a movie for your favorite actor?

714. Meet your favorite singer and not be able to speak ←or→ meet a singer you hate but be able to talk a mile a minute?

715. Attend a party with your favorite celebrity but not be able to talk to them ←or→ get a signed photo in the mail from your favorite celebrity?

716. Be the president of a celebrity's fan club ←or→ have a celebrity be president of your fan club?

717. Meet your favorite author but not get your book signed ←or→ get an autographed book but no meeting?

718. Take a picture with a celebrity ←or→ get their autograph?

719. Have your favorite celebrity's phone number ←or→ your favorite celebrity's address?

720. Get free delivery but you never choose the meal ←or→
choose the meal but it costs twice as much as normal?

721. Win a bronze medal in a sport you love ←or→
a gold medal in a sport you hate?

722. Have your own messy desk ←or→ a shared neat desk?

723. Eat only sweet snacks forever ←or→ salty snacks forever?

724. Walk the Great Wall of China ←or→ the Appian Way?

725. Race the Iditarod ←or→ swim the English Channel?

726. Visit the North Pole ←or→ the South Pole?

727. Climb Mount Everest ←or→ explore the Mariana Trench?

728. See the Great Pyramids ←or→ the Grand Canyon?

729. Be kissed on the beach ←or→ in the rain?

730. Get married on the beach ←or→ in the mountains?

731. Be a horse that no one loves ←or→ a spider that is beloved?

732. Be a roach and stay with your loved ones forever ←or→
a puppy but everyone hates you?

733. Run a triathlon ←or→ compete in a biathlon?

734. In baseball, never strike out ←or→ always get walked?

735. Get slapped by someone you love ←or→ kissed by someone you hate?

736. Be ugly with beautiful hair ←or→ beautiful with terrible hair?

737. Get free pedicures for life but never pick the color ←or→ expensive pedicures but you always pick the color?

738. Poke a wasp's nest ←or→ step on a sleeping rattlesnake?

739. Be great at a board game you hate and bad at everything else ←or→ good at everything but terrible at a board game you love?

740. Peel a banana ←or→ peel an orange?

741. Eat too many carrots ←or→ too much broccoli?

742. Go barefoot on concrete ←or→ wear big boots in the grass?

743. Be able to catch all the prizes in the claw machine but never take them home ←or→ always win at air hockey but never get to be on the leaderboard?

744. Eat noodles ←or→ rice?

745. Roller skate to work ←or→ ski to school?

746. Never learn to ride a bike ←or→ never learn to swim?

747. Slow dance to a fast song ←or→ fast dance to a slow song?

748. At concerts, participate in a mosh pit ←or→ a wall of death?

749. Be in the audience of a music awards show ←or→ a movie award show?

750. Perform with a boyband ←or→ interview a boyband?

751. Get a massage that feels bad ←or→ a pedicure you hate?

752. Be amazing at a skill you hate ←or→ just okay at a skill you love?

753. Be tickled for three hours ←or→ pinched for three minutes?

754. Get a tattoo of something you hate ←or→ shave your head?

755. Lick the bottom of a boot ←or→ a dog's nose?

756. Wear acid-washed jeans ←or→ bellbottoms?

757. Listen to EDM on repeat ←or→ country on repeat?

758. Break all your bones at once ←or→ one bone every day for 206 days?

759. Have a dog that meows ←or→ a cat that barks?

760. Have a neck like a giraffe ←or→ a trunk like an elephant?

761. Quack like a duck ←or→ chirp like a canary?

762. Meet the love of your life but they can't understand your language ←or→ be perfectly understood by someone you hate?

763. Splash in a mud puddle ←or→ take a bath in whipped cream?

764. Have a delicious burned steak ←or→ a terrible rare steak?

765. Get free desserts for life ←or→ free appetizers for life?

766. Get free clothes for life ←or→ free beauty products for life?

767. Drive your dream car for one day ←or→ a car you hate for one year?

768. Be bored at work for little money ←or→
productive at work for lots of money?

769. Only speak in rhymes ←or→ in songs?

770. Only speak in coughs ←or→ in burps?

771. Sneeze every time you had an embarrassing thought ←or→
cough every time you thought about your crush?

772. Send an email that takes two weeks to arrive ←or→
a snail mail letter that takes two days to arrive?

773. Have unlimited sick time but no vacation time ←or→
unlimited vacation time but no sick days?

774. Snow ski ←or→ jet ski?

775. Dive for pearls ←or→ mine for diamonds?

776. Wear dentures ←or→ a wig?

777. Play basketball ←or→ baseball?

778. Play the guitar badly ←or→ the banjo well?

779. Be a famous conductor ←or→ a famous showrunner?

780. Shop online but everything is extra expensive ←or→ shop in person but everything is super cheap?

781. Get caught cheating on a person ←or→ cheating on an exam?

782. Get caught with your pants down in public ←or→ picking your nose in public?

783. Frame your BFF for a crime ←or→ get framed by the police for a crime?

784. Rescue a kitten from a tree ←or→ a dog from the street?

785. Have stinky breath ←or→ stinky feet?

786. Get free tools for life but they always break ←or→ pay double for really good, reliable tools?

787. Hardwood floors ←or→ carpet?

788. Wallpaper ←or→ painted walls?

789. Sleep on memory foam ←or→ a waterbed?

790. A blizzard in the summer ←or→ a heat wave in the winter?

791. Live in fall forever ←or→ spring forever?

792. One, big rain for 40 hours ←or→ one hour of rain for 40 days?

793. Free food but you have to put hot sauce on everything ←or→ you pay double for food seasoned just as you like?

794. Read 30 books in one day ←or→ read one book for 30 days?

795. Skip college but have a guaranteed good job ←or→
go to college with no employment after?

796. Learn a trade ←or→ get a degree?

797. Receive free college but you don't get to pick your major ←or→
a well-playing job but you're assigned to it?

798. Rule a dystopia ←or→ a utopia?

799. Have a cat pounce on your toes with its claws out ←or→
step on a push pin?

800. Have soft skin ←or→ silky hair?

801. Grow a moustache but no beard ←or→ a beard but no moustache?

802. Backpack ←or→ messenger bag?

803. Wallet ←or→ a money clip?

804. Check time on your phone ←or→ on a watch?

805. Study at the library ←or→ at a coffee shop?

806. Get spam email ←or→ junk mail?

807. Travel to a faraway star ←or→ a faraway planet?

808. Live your entire life on a spaceship ←or→ on a submarine?

809. Walk on stilts ←or→ ride a unicycle?

810. Eat deep dish pizza ←or→ thin crust pizza?

811. Be read a bedtime story ←or→ sung a lullaby?

812. Have beautiful hair ←or→ beautiful clothes?

813. Wear beautiful clothes ←or→ beautiful jewelry?

814. Collect expensive shoes ←or→ expensive handbags?

815. Be rich but have bad acne ←or→ have clear skin but no money?

816. Wristwatch ←or→ pocket watch?

817. Eat terrible chocolate chip cookies ←or→ delicious oatmeal raisin cookies?

818. Be remembered ←or→ forgotten?

819. Undo a big, public mistake ←or→ make several tiny mistakes that go unnoticed?

820. Decorate for Christmas ←or→ for Halloween?

821. Use a word processor ←or→ a typewriter?

822. Build databases ←or→ spreadsheets?

823. Only listen to your favorite song ←or→ never hear your favorite song again?

824. Only watch your favorite movie ←or→ never see your favorite movie again?

825. Celebrate all your birthdays at once ←or→ have everyone forget your birthday every year?

826. Everyone forget your face ←or→ your name?

827. Read a good book but not remember it ←or→ read a terrible book and remember everything?

828. Free groceries for life ←or→ free clothes for life?

829. Free shoes that don't match any of your clothes ←or→ free clothes that don't match any of your shoes?

830. Sunburned in the winter ←or→ frostbitten in the summer?

831. Ride the scariest roller coaster in the world ←or→ never ever ride a roller coaster?

832. Drive a car ←or→ fly a plane?

833. Nap in the day but have a bad night's sleep ←or→ have a good night's sleep and stay awake all day?

834. Eat a fried cake ←or→ a cream filled chicken nugget?

835. Be awakened by a horn honk every hour ←or→ never sleep because of a constant horn honk?

836. Be stuck in traffic in a big city ←or→ drive unhindered along a boring country road?

837. Drink spoiled milk but never get sick ←or→ drink okay milk but always get sick?

838. Be a baby knowing all you know now ←or→ be an adult but know nothing?

839. Bring a loved one back from the dead for a day ←or→ change one moment in time?

840. Live in a solitary prison ←or→ in a cult?

841. Live one year on Mars ←or→ be homeless for a year?

842. Eat an entire onion ←or→ eat an entire garlic bulb?

843. Drink onion juice ←or→ drink garlic juice?

844. Travel to the future but lose ten years of your life ←or→ go back to the past and gain ten years of your life?

845. Trade years of your life for magic ←or→ trade magic for more years of life?

846. Have your crush read your diary ←or→ go through your text messages?

847. Have one boring year with the love of your life ←or→ 10 amazing years with someone you only sort of like?

848. Live in Austin ←or→ Los Angeles?

849. Wait 10 years to get $5 million ←or→ get $10,000 right now?

850. Be able to walk on your hands ←or→ do backflips?

851. Take a free trip to your favorite theme park but you have to buy all your food ←or→ get free food at your favorite theme park but you have to pay for the trip?

852. Meet your soulmate once and never see them again ←or→ never meet your soulmate in the first place?

853. Never forget ←or→ always remember?

854. Be busted for something you didn't do ←or→ blamed for something you did do?

855. Eat the middle of brownies ←or→ the corners?

856. Have your pizza cut into triangles ←or→ cut into squares?

857. Tell your mother your most embarrassing moment ←or→ tell your crush your most embarrassing moment?

858. Do karaoke in front of your crush ←or→ have a dance contest against your crush?

859. Wear winter clothes in summer ←or→ summer clothes in winter?

860. Go on a cruise with someone you hate ←or→ stay in a hostel with someone you love?

861. Drink hot chocolate with marshmallows ←or→ with whipped cream?

862. Your parents embarrass you with your old baby pictures ←or→ with old stories about you?

863. Get pooped on by a bird ←or→ step in dog poop on the street?

864. Get sprayed by a skunk ←or→ puked on by a cat?

865. Brush your teeth with coal ←or→ take a shower in paint?

866. Carry an umbrella but it never rains ←or→ never carry an umbrella but it always rains?

867. Get pulled over for going too fast ←or→ for going too slow?

868. Fanny pack ←or→ cargo pants?

869. Tan easily ←or→ lose weight easily?

870. Only be able to shop online ←or→ never be able to shop online again?

871. Disappoint your parents ←or→ your significant other?

872. Slide down a giant noodle ←or→ a giant celery stick?

873. Dance with a snake ←or→ cuddle with a scorpion?

874. Eat raw steak ←or→ burned popcorn?

875. Pee every time you sneeze ←or→ fart every time you cough?

876. Commute five hours a day for a good-paying job ←or→ work from home for a job that pays poorly?

877. Work in an office for three days a week ←or→ work from home seven days a week?

878. Crack a raw egg on your forehead ←or→ fall in front of your friends?

879. Participate in the modern Olympics ←or→ the ancient Olympics?

880. Get caught lying to your parents ←or→ to your spouse?

881. Be able to hear like a bat ←or→ catch scents like a dog?

882. Become famous acting in a movie you hate ←or→ stay small time but acting in a movie you love?

883. Have a picnic at the beach ←or→ a picnic at the mountains?

884. Be super wealthy with no friends ←or→ family ←or→ poor but surrounded by love?

885. Have infinite money ←or→ infinite knowledge?

886. Fame ←or→ power?

887. Wealth ←or→ power?

888. Rich and weak ←or→ poor and strong?

889. Be the rescuer ←or→ the rescued?

890. Comic books ←or→ graphic novels?

891. Speak only in movie quotes ←or→ in poems?

892. Be stuck in an elevator ←or→ underground in a subway car?

893. Sightsee in Africa ←or→ shop in Milan?

894. Bungee jump ←or→ sky dive?

895. Own a famous hotel ←or→ a famous airline?

896. Get caught in an avalanche ←or→ a hurricane?

897. Dance in a ballet ←or→ sing in a musical?

898. Be a bestselling author ←or→ an award-winning singer?

899. Be an award-winning actor ←or→ a beloved philanthropist?

900. Have a bestselling book but no one knows you wrote it ←or→ an OK selling book but everyone knows you're the author?

901. Face your worst fear ←or→ confess your worst sins?

902. Confess your sins online ←or→ face to face?

903. Give up coffee ←or→ not brush your teeth for a year?

904. Wear yellow every day ←or→ never wear jewelry?

905. Write the best book ever but no one reads it ←or→ write a bad book but everyone reads it?

906. Act on a soap opera ←or→ be a talk show host?

907. Direct a soap opera ←or→ produce a game show?

908. Eat soap ←or→ wash with toothpaste?

909. Go to an amusement park ←or→ a water park?

910. Soak in a hot tub ←or→ in a hot spring?

911. Float in the Dead Sea ←or→ surf off the coast of Australia?

912. Risk it all for love ←or→ risk it all for success?

913. Be successful in business ←or→ successful in love?

914. Date someone unattractive but mean ←or→ nice but unattractive?

915. Live a comfortable boring life ←or→ an exciting unstable life?

916. Take vitamins ←or→ eat vegetables?

917. Eat tasty food that is bad for you ←or→ nasty food that is good for you?

918. Be a boss working 80 hours a week ←or→ an individual contributor working 40 hours a week?

919. Be an A-list actor but all of your film shoots are in Siberia ←or→ a C-list actor but all your shoots are in Maui?

920. Have a beautiful singing voice ←or→ a body that can dance to any song?

921. Autobiographies ←or→ biographies?

922. Interview regular people on a talk show ←or→ famous people on a radio show?

923. Be reincarnated as a dog ←or→ a cat?

924. Be reincarnated as a bird ←or→ a fish?

925. Cure cancer ←or→ cure the common cold?

926. Be an organ donor ←or→ donate your body to science?

927. Have perfect teeth ←or→ perfect hair?

928. Have perfect posture ←or→ perfect skin?

929. Mullet ←or→ cornrows?

930. Lip gloss ←or→ lipstick?

931. Wired headphones ←or→ wireless earbuds?

932. Find a rare fossil ←or→ genuine gold?

933. Wear a giant fake diamond ←or→ a tiny real diamond?

934. Own a mansion ←or→ an expensive car?

935. Be a wizard ←or→ a god?

936. Have super powers ←or→ magical powers?

937. Date an actor ←or→ a musician?

938. Date a rock star ←or→ a movie star?

939. Date a doctor ←or→ a lawyer?

940. Have a big house with no furniture ←or→ a small house with loads of furniture?

941. Be fast ←or→ smart?

942. Kiss a roach ←or→ a spider?

943. Be a frog ←or→ a toad?

944. Broccoli ←or→ cauliflower?

945. Carrots ←or→ radishes?

946. Be a great speaker ←or→ a great singer?

947. Be charming ←or→ good looking?

948. Hard shell ←or→ soft shell tacos?

949. Burritos ←or→ enchiladas?

950. Spaghetti ←or→ lasagna?

951. Have cramps for five days ←or→ migraines for five days?

952. Have a natural childbirth ←or→ a tooth extraction with no painkillers?

953. Break your toe ←or→ your finger?

954. Fish sticks ←or→ chicken nuggets?

955. Chunky peanut butter ←or→ creamy peanut butter?

956. Be in a secret society ←or→ go on a secret mission?

957. Work for minimum wage ←or→ be a panhandler?

958. Swim in a pool ←or→ swim in the ocean?

959. Ride in an airplane ←or→ on a helicopter?

960. Spit when you talk ←or→ fart when you walk?

961. Be bribed ←or→ blackmailed?

962. Travel the world in a hot air balloon ←or→ walk across your country?

963. Sing karaoke ←or→ recite a poem?

964. Give a speech in front of 500 people ←or→
sing karaoke in front of 100 people?

965. Listen to jazz ←or→ blues?

966. Be a ballet dancer ←or→ a modern dancer?

967. Be in a music video ←or→ sing backup for a famous singer?

968. Track and field ←or→ gymnastics?

969. Be on TV ←or→ do a livestream?

970. Forget your lines in a play ←or→ forget all the answers for a test?

971. Bloom like a flower ←or→ root down like a tree?

972. Use a film camera ←or→ a digital camera?

973. Hear ←or→ see?

974. Shave your head ←or→ dye your hair a color you hate?

975. Give up social media for a week ←or→ all technology for a month?

976. Date someone 20 years older than you ←or→ 20 years younger than you?

977. French fries ←or→ sweet potato fries?

978. Go on a cruise ←or→ a train ride?

979. Work four 10-hour days ←or→ 10 four-hour days?

980. Burn candles ←or→ burn incense?

981. Learn to knit ←or→ crochet?

982. Learn needlepoint ←or→ embroidery?

983. Have stuffed animals ←or→ live pets?

984. Pet a python ←or→ a boa constrictor?

985. Mice ←or→ rats?

986. Pigeons ←or→ turtle doves?

987. Be a turtle ←or→ a tortoise?

988. Have fully charged electronics forever ←or→ free internet forever?

989. Solar eclipse ←or→ a lunar eclipse?

990. Fountain pens ←or→ a ballpoint pens?

991. Lead pencils ←or→ a mechanical pencils?

992. Tie-dye your hair ←or→ tie-dye your clothes?

993. Cow's milk ←or→ goat's milk?

994. Cow cheese ←or→ goat cheese?

995. Get gum on your face ←or→ gum in your hair?

996. Meditate for two hours ←or→ read for two hours?

997. Do 100 sit-ups ←or→ 100 pushups?

998. Eat your least favorite food ←or→ drink your least favorite drink?

999. Never shower again ←or→ never brush your teeth again?

1000. Stand in line for 15 minutes with a full bladder ←or→ use a filthy bathroom immediately?

1001. Skydive ←or→ swim with sharks?

1002. Get stung by a bee ←or→ stung by a jellyfish?

1003. Be allergic to flowers ←or→ allergic to grass?

1004. Be allergic to peanuts ←or→ allergic to shellfish?

1005. Be president ←or→ prime minister?

1006. Ramen ←or→ udon?

1007. Be popular ←or→ have your privacy?

1008. Be exhausted and happy ←or→ well-rested and sad?

1009. Sleep in the woods ←or→ on the beach?

1010. Get chased by a bear ←or→ a lion?

1011. Buy ←or→ rent an apartment?

1012. Buy ←or→ rent a house?

1013. Go to the library ←or→ a bookstore?

1014. Listen to punk ←or→ heavy metal?

1015. Take a photo ←or→ pose for a photo?

1016. Use a laptop ←or→ a smartphone?

1017. Have big feet and small hands ←or→ small feet and big hands?

1018. Do something nice for someone you can't stand ←or→
do something mean to someone you adore?

1019. Lick a frog ←or→ kiss a roach?

1020. Eat pig's feet ←or→ chicken feet?

1021. Trip and fall in front of your crush ←or→ trip in front of a crowd?

1022. Tell your crush you like them ←or→ confess to cheating on a test?

1023. Be a vampire ←or→ a vampire hunter?

1024. Be just friends with a crush ←or→ have a crush on your best friend?

1025. Live alone in your dream home ←or→ date someone you aren't really into?

1026. Be a ruler with little money ←or→ a citizen with a lot of money?

1027. Ride on horseback ←or→ in a rickshaw?

1028. Ride in a carriage ←or→ in a rickshaw?

1029. Walk alone down a dark street at night ←or→
walk through an angry mob in broad daylight?

1030. Eat a dead worm ←or→ a live cicada?

1031. Play it safe and have regrets ←or→ take chances and have no regrets?

1032. Live forever with little energy ←or→ have a lot of energy but only a few months to live?

1033. Walk for a mile on your hands ←or→ crawl for a mile on your knees?

1034. Be good at what you hate ←or→ bad at what you love?

1035. Have no emotions ←or→ have no taste?

1036. Have dinner with your favorite author ←or→ your favorite singer?

1037. Be able to look but not touch ←or→ touch without looking?

1038. Meet with your favorite celebrity for five minutes ←or→ vacation with your best friend for five days?

1039. Wet your pants in public ←or→ trip and fall in public?

1040. Cookie dough ←or→ cake batter?

1041. Chips ←or→ crackers?

1042. Dill pickles ←or→ sweet pickles?

1043. Corned beef ←or→ pastrami?

1044. Run uphill on ice ←or→ slide downhill on sharp rocks?

1045. Live in a rainforest ←or→ live in a desert?

1046. Be trapped in a haunted house ←or→ an enchanted forest?

1047. Elf ←or→ dwarf?

1048. Ogre ←or→ troll?

1049. Learn a new language ←or→ learn a new musical instrument?

1050. Have no rhythm ←or→ be tone deaf?

1051. Make a snow angel ←or→ build a snow fort?

1052. Grow a flower garden ←or→ a vegetable garden?

1053. Build a sand castle ←or→ a snow fort?

1054. Live in Alaska for free ←or→ in Hawaii for 10% over the normal cost?

1055. Be a famous college athlete ←or→ an unknown pro athlete?

1056. Never sleep with a blanket ←or→ never sleep with a pillow

1057. Sleep on a bed of nails ←or→ on a bed of coals?

1058. Milkshakes ←or→ root beer floats?

1059. Bathe in sour milk ←or→ shower in nacho cheese?

1060. Eat lunch with someone you hate ←or→ starve alone?

1061. Find out your favorite celebrity is not nice ←or→
find out your sworn enemy is your soulmate?

1062. Have your favorite TV show cancelled ←or→
your favorite book series never get the next part?

1063. Bike with no helmet ←or→ deep sea dive with no scuba gear?

1064. Hit an iceberg ←or→ get sucked down a giant drain?

1065. Spend a night with spiders ←or→ with snakes?

1066. Eat pizza with only veggies ←or→ never eat pizza again?

1067. Have spinach in your teeth ←or→ a stain on your shirt?

1068. Interview a politician ←or→ a celebrity?

1069. Lose your sense of smell ←or→ sense of taste?

1070. Get trapped in a maze ←or→ in a cave?

1071. New clothes ←or→ new shoes?

1072. Cook dinner ←or→ wash the dishes?

1073. Sort and wash the laundry ←or→ fold and put away the laundry?

1074. Pick up after your dog ←or→ scoop out the cat's litter box?

1075. Chaperone your son ←or→ chaperone your daughter?

1076. Control the weather ←or→ predict the future?

1077. Golden Retriever ←or→ Yellow Labrador?

1078. Fried fish ←or→ baked fish?

1079. Soy milk ←or→ almond milk?

1080. Cereal with milk ←or→ dry?

1081. Date your best friend ←or→ marry your worst enemy?

1082. Sleep in a comfortable bed that is too small ←or→ a spacious bed that is uncomfortable?

1083. Have a year-long stomachache ←or→ a year-long headache?

1084. Be nearsighted ←or→ farsighted?

1085. Wear glasses ←or→ contacts?

1086. Play checkers ←or→ chess?

1087. Be popular with bad grades ←or→ unpopular with good grades?

1088. Wear a skirt on a windy day ←or→ wear long pants on a hot day?

1089. Do public speaking ←or→ be locked in solitary confinement?

1090. Crossword puzzles ←or→ word search puzzles?

1091. Have your house smell like herbs ←or→ smell like spices?

1092. Collect stamps ←or→ stickers?

1093. Bite your tongue ←or→ bite your lip?

1094. Be a soldier ←or→ a wizard?

1095. Follow the rules ←or→ make your own rules?

1096. Tennis ←or→ polo?

1097. Horse race ←or→ a car race?

1098. Get caught in a downpour ←or→ in a blizzard?

1099. Be a magician ←or→ a singer?

1100. Be a character in a mystery book ←or→ in a romance novel?

1101. Bump your head ←or→ stub your toe?

1102. Party with people you hate ←or→ sit home alone?

1103. Start your own business ←or→ buy someone else's business?

1104. Super speed ←or→ super hearing?

1105. Meet a talking scarecrow ←or→ a singing lion?

1106. Have a food fight ←or→ a snowball fight?

1107. Never have to wait in line ←or→ never have to search for a parking space?

1108. Travel at the speed of light ←or→ travel at the speed of sound?

1109. Tell ghost stories ←or→ have ghosts tell stories about you?

1110. Be able to predict the future ←or→ fix the past?

1111. Be bowlegged ←or→ knock-kneed?

1112. Hummus ←or→ salsa?

1113. Wear a swimsuit to a wedding ←or→ a wedding dress to a pool?

1114. Brush your hair with your toothbrush ←or→
brush your teeth with your hairbrush?

1115. Get locked out of your car ←or→ locked out of your house?

1116. Gray hair ←or→ wrinkles?

1117. Eat dinner with your ex ←or→ dessert with your enemy?

1118. Take a nap ←or→ go for a walk?

1119. Find a four-leaf clover ←or→ a rabbit's foot?

1120. Have only good luck for a week ←or→ only bad luck for an hour?

1121. Start a rumor ←or→ have a rumor started about you?

1122. Watch reality TV ←or→ be on reality TV?

1123. Hollywood movies ←or→ Bollywood movies?

1124. Play in the rain ←or→ play in the snow?

1125. Swim in a lake ←or→ swim in a river?

1126. Live in a tiny house ←or→ live in a mansion?

1127. Organize your house ←or→ organize someone else's house?

1128. Have thick, short hair ←or→ thin, long hair?

1129. Have hair that grows fast ←or→ nails that grow fast?

1130. Have a bushy beard ←or→ bushy eyebrows?

1131. Have a loud voice ←or→ a soft voice?

1132. Have a high-pitched voice ←or→ a low-pitched voice?

1133. Be the judge ←or→ jury?

1134. Be wrong ←or→ right?

1135. Free haircuts ←or→ free clothes?

1136. Report your lover for committing a crime ←or→ take the blame?

1137. Cheddar cheese ←or→ muenster cheese?

1138. Live next door to a cemetery ←or→ a morgue?

1139. Leather seats ←or→ cloth seats?

1140. Sleep on the floor ←or→ share a bed with all of your siblings?

1141. Eat dinner too early ←or→ eat dinner too late?

1142. Rainstorms ←or→ snowstorms?

1143. Sleep on the ground when camping ←or→ sleep on a cot?

1144. Use an outhouse ←or→ dig a hole?

1145. Meet a bear ←or→ a mountain lion in the woods?

1146. Be the voice of reason ←or→ throw caution to the wind?

1147. Be a team player ←or→ a team leader?

1148. Manage an unruly team that wins ←or→ a good-natured team that loses?

1149. Host a morning show ←or→ host a late-night show?

1150. Be a deer running from a human hunter ←or→ a mouse running from a cat?

1151. Candle ←or→ flashlight?

1152. Umbrella ←or→ raincoat?

1153. Long days and short nights ←or→ short days and long nights?

1154. Be a school nurse ←or→ a hospital nurse?

1155. Pharmacist ←or→ a doctor?

1156. Sleep next to someone who snores ←or→ talks in their sleep?

1157. Wood floors ←or→ cement floors?

1158. Linoleum ←or→ tile?

1159. CDs ←or→ vinyl?

1160. Lose an unhealthy amount of weight ←or→ gain an unhealthy amount of weight?

1161. Drink too much ←or→ eat too much?

1162. Go 30 days without music ←or→ 30 days without TV?

1163. Be a librarian ←or→ a bookseller?

1164. Discover oil ←or→ gold?

1165. Find diamonds ←or→ silver?

1166. Be good at math ←or→ good at sports?

1167. Be worshipped ←or→ appreciated?

1168. Be good at tennis ←or→ good at golf?

1169. Hot apple cider ←or→ hot cocoa?

1170. Apple pie ←or→ pumpkin pie?

1171. Sweat pants ←or→ leggings?

1172. Yoga ←or→ Pilates?

1173. Glee club ←or→ choir?

1174. Be made out of cake ←or→ made out of meat?

1175. Peel potatoes ←or→ chop onions?

1176. Peanuts ←or→ walnuts?

1177. Candy with nuts ←or→ candy with fruit?

1178. Brownies with nuts ←or→ extra chocolate/fudge?

1179. Full-size donuts ←or→ donut holes?

1180. Is the glass half empty ←or→ half full?

1181. Buried alive ←or→ handcuffed under water?

1182. Butter popcorn ←or→ kettle corn?

1183. Be mentally healthy ←or→ physically healthy?

1184. Be cutthroat ←or→ moral?

1185. Have a famous child ←or→ a famous parent?

1186. Go on a safari ←or→ go on a cruise?

1187. Be a cheerleader ←or→ a football player?

1188. Be in the circus ←or→ work at a zoo?

1189. Have a pet manticore ←or→ a pet dire wolf?

1190. Be a goblin ←or→ a nymph?

1191. Be a sorceress ←or→ a soothsayer?

1192. Be a rebel outlaw ←or→ a brave knight?

1193. Have dinner with your favorite actor ←or→ your favorite author?

1194. Be best friends with an alien ←or→ best friends with a mermaid?

1195. Play Truth or Dare with your parents ←or→ Would You Rather with your siblings?

1196. Smell like a rose ←or→ smell like an orange?

1197. Be short and cute ←or→ tall and beautiful?

1198. Win a wrestling match ←or→ a boxing match?

1199. Plan a trip in advance ←or→ take off at the last minute?

1200. Pack for vacation a week in advance ←or→
throw everything together the day of the flight?

1201. Text all night ←or→ talk on the phone for 10 minutes?

1202. Go bowling ←or→ play pool?

1203. Go to a nightclub ←or→ a concert?

1204. Go camping ←or→ go to a theme park?

1205. Cake ←or→ pie for breakfast?

1206. Be friends with a witch ←or→ a fairy?

1207. Wish on a star ←or→ find a four-leaf clover?

1208. Lose your passport ←or→ lose your driver's license?

1209. Forget how to drive ←or→ forget how to ride a bike?

1210. Stay up until 5am ←or→ sleep until 9pm?

1211. Read a 500-page book ←or→ read five 100-page books?

1212. Paper planners ←or→ electronic planners?

1213. Stickers ←or→ rubber stamps?

1214. Sleep with a teddy bear ←or→ a security blanket?

1215. Suck your thumb ←or→ bite your nails?

1216. Only eat junk food ←or→ never eat junk food?

1217. Bat ←or→ bird?

1218. Be a ruler everyone hates ←or→ a civilian everyone loves?

1219. Lose your hearing ←or→ your hair?

1220. Lose your wedding ring ←or→ your wallet?

1221. Give up French fries ←or→ cheeseburgers?

1222. Give up alcohol ←or→ soda?

1223. Eat ice cream but it always gives you brain freeze ←or→ drink coffee but it always burns your tongue?

1224. Hot tub ←or→ pool?

1225. Live by a lake ←or→ a river?

1226. Have 70 cars ←or→ a mansion?

1227. Be woken up by beeping ←or→ by music?

1228. Take a shower in the morning ←or→ at night?

1229. Wash the dishes ←or→ clean the toilet?

1230. Exercise outdoors ←or→ go to the gym?

1231. Jog ←or→ power walk?

1232. Run a marathon ←or→ a 5K?

1233. Exercise in the morning ←or→ in the evening?

1234. Go fishing ←or→ go hunting?

1235. Stargaze under the sky ←or→ go to a planetarium?

1236. Watch football on TV ←or→ at a stadium?

1237. Watch a concert on TV and get great views ←or→ watch a concert live but be far away from the stage?

1238. Whipped cream ←or→ hot fudge?

1239. Sprinkles ←or→ nuts?

1240. Super speed ←or→ super strength?

1241. Never sweat ←or→ never be hungry?

1242. Never need a haircut ←or→ never need to shower?

1243. Boxers ←or→ briefs?

1244. Sweaty palms ←or→ sweaty armpits?

1245. Meet a vampire ←or→ a zombie?

1246. Date a werewolf ←or→ a vampire?

1247. Date a fairy ←or→ a princess?

1248. Date an elf ←or→ a prince?

1249. Date a fairy ←or→ an elf?

1250. Be king ←or→ magician?

1251. Live in a castle ←or→ a palace?

1252. Have a maid ←or→ a chauffeur?

1253. Get cheated on ←or→ be the cheater?

1254. Be the dumper ←or→ the dumpee?

1255. Give up salt ←or→ sugar forever?

1256. Hot drinks ←or→ cold drinks?

1257. Hot sandwiches ←or→ cold sandwiches?

1258. Fruit pies ←or→ a meat pies?

1259. Bacon for dinner ←or→ chicken for breakfast?

1260. Pizza with anchovies ←or→ no pizza forever?

1261. Eat alone ←or→ don't eat at all?

1262. The school meatloaf ←or→ the school tuna fish?

1263. Give up social media ←or→ texting?

1264. Give up the Internet ←or→ music?

1265. Give up shopping ←or→ TV?

1266. Climb a mountain ←or→ parachute from a plane?

1267. Tour a celebrity's home ←or→ an ancient church?

1268. Shop in New York City ←or→ shop in Paris?

1269. Dimples ←or→ freckles?

1270. Big teeth ←or→ a big nose?

1271. Small eyes ←or→ small ears?

1272. Visit the zoo ←or→ go on a safari?

1273. Raise tropical fish ←or→ salt-water fish?

1274. Raise chickens ←or→ pigs?

1275. Grow corn ←or→ soybeans?

1276. Shave your legs ←or→ wax your eyebrows?

1277. Live in a gingerbread house ←or→ a candy house?

1278. Live in a glass house ←or→ a metal house?

1279. Take the elevator ←or→ take the stairs?

1280. Live in a big city ←or→ a small town?

1281. Get 40 splinters at once ←or→ a splinter a day for 40 days?

1282. Go to a tea party ←or→ a birthday party?

1283. Go to a frat party ←or→ a costume party?

1284. Have tea with the queen of England ←or→ dinner with your favorite actor?

1285. Chocolate milk ←or→ hot chocolate?

1286. Orange juice ←or→ grape juice?

1287. Apple juice ←or→ apple cider?

1288. Go on a hayride ←or→ play in a pumpkin patch?

1289. Sleep in a barn ←or→ sleep in a strange bed?

1290. Get lost in the woods ←or→ lost in the mountains?

1291. Build a snowman ←or→ splash in a puddle?

1292. Make paper snowflakes ←or→ paper airplanes?

1293. Draw pictures ←or→ play games?

1294. Do arts and crafts ←or→ watch TV?

1295. Forget how to talk ←or→ forget how to write?

1296. Fall asleep at work ←or→ fall asleep at church?

1297. Watch football ←or→ baseball?

1298. Be sweaty and cold ←or→ itchy and hot?

1299. Visit China ←or→ Japan?

1300. Visit Ireland ←or→ Scotland?

1301. Visit Spain ←or→ Portugal?

1302. Visit the United States ←or→ Canada?

1303. Be a robot ←or→ an alien?

1304. Party with your friends ←or→ snuggle with your crush?

1305. Get a back rub ←or→ a foot massage?

1306. Get acupuncture ←or→ go to the chiropractor?

1307. Get a flu shot ←or→ get a tooth filling?

1308. Paper checks ←or→ direct deposit?

1309. Float like a butterfly ←or→ sting like a bee?

1310. Drop a gallon of milk ←or→ an open bottle of pills?

1311. Ice hockey ←or→ field hockey?

1312. Softball ←or→ baseball?

1313. Lose your medicine ←or→ lose your keys?

1314. Ice skate ←or→ roller skate?

1315. Wear a helmet ←or→ knee pads?

1316. Plastic surgery ←or→ brain surgery?

1317. Costume party ←or→ a masquerade ball?

1318. Operas ←or→ musicals?

1319. Slow dance at a night club ←or→ fast dance at a party?

1320. Text on your phone ←or→ chat on your computer?

1321. Be a famous author ←or→ famous on social media?

1322. Work with lots of money but never touch it ←or→ have lots of money but never spend it?

1323. Have the speed of a cheetah ←or→ the strength of a lion?

1324. Lavender ←or→ rosemary?

1325. Cook with all spices except salt ←or→ only cook with salt?

1326. Go to a carnival ←or→ a circus?

1327. Go to a fortune teller ←or→ a bank teller?

1328. Ride the tallest roller coaster ←or→ the fastest roller coaster?

1329. Celebrate only your favorite holiday ←or→ only your birthday?

1330. Grow old but never die ←or→ get stuck the age you are but die in 20 years?

1331. Sledding ←or→ snowboarding?

1332. Ride in a ski lift ←or→ a helicopter?

1333. Deep sea diving ←or→ white water rafting?

1334. Air conditioning ←or→ fans?

1335. Drive with the air conditioning on ←or→ with the windows down?

1336. Radio ←or→ streaming service?

1337. Drive ←or→ ride a train across the country?

1338. Be stuck behind a slow truck ←or→ be tailed by a police car?

1339. Be stuck behind a school bus that stops on every block ←or→ stuck in a one-hour traffic jam?

1340. Be a nurse ←or→ a doctor?

1341. Be a guidance counselor ←or→ a psychiatrist?

1342. Work at a boutique ←or→ a discount store?

1343. Buy new groceries every day ←or→ once a week?

1344. Bake fresh bread every day ←or→ buy packaged bread every week?

1345. Tell your crush how you feel ←or→ confess to a transgression you didn't commit?

1346. Over-the-ear headphones with no wires ←or→ ear buds with wires?

1347. Popcorn with sugar ←or→ candy with salt?

1348. Visit Iceland ←or→ Greenland?

1349. Get caught in a lightning storm ←or→ a hailstorm?

1350. Be in an earthquake ←or→ a hurricane?

1351. Give up ice cream ←or→ give up cheese?

1352. Wear pink ←or→ blue forever?

1353. Spend only one year with the love of your life ←or→
spend the rest of your life with someone you like but don't love?

1354. Be an author on a book tour ←or→ a singer on a concert tour?

1355. Date your crush but never kiss them ←or→
date your enemy but always kiss them?

1356. Take amazing photos only in black and white ←or→
color photos but they're just OK?

1357. Watch a film with no talking ←or→ one with no music?

1358. Have unlimited free time but no money ←or→
unlimited money but no free time?

1359. Sleep with a comfortable pillow ←or→ on a comfortable mattress?

1360. Camp in the woods ←or→ on the beach?

1361. Swim with a dolphin ←or→ run with a giraffe?

1362. Have a pet kangaroo ←or→ a pet emu?

1363. Only have dull razers ←or→ dull knives?

1364. Only play your favorite game forever ←or→ be able to play any other game for free?

1365. Live in an igloo ←or→ a straw house?

1366. Live in Russia for a year ←or→ Bermuda for a week?

1367. Drink tea with no sugar ←or→ coffee with no cream?

1368. Date your favorite celebrity ←or→ date your soul mate?

1369. Shave your head ←or→ shave your eyebrows?

1370. Get paid to play video games ←or→ paid to shop?

1371. Get a parking ticket ←or→ a speeding ticket?

1372. Give up your dishwasher ←or→ your microwave?

1373. Spy on a criminal ←or→ on your boss?

1374. Have a messy desk and a clear mind ←or→ a clear desk and a messy mind?

1375. Bathe your dog ←or→ bathe your cat?

1376. Pet a minotaur ←or→ a werewolf?

1377. Have a pet Pegasus ←or→ a pet satyr?

1378. Have a gnome in your garden ←or→ a flamingo in your yard?

1379. Answer a riddle from a troll ←or→ a sphinx?

1380. Be a devil ←or→ an angel on a shoulder?

1381. Be a good writer ←or→ a good singer?

1382. Eat a cricket flavored lollipop ←or→ a lollipop flavored cricket?

1383. Have super vision ←or→ super hearing?

1384. Be athletic ←or→ smart?

1385. Solve the meaning of life ←or→ know what happens after you die?

1386. Be a dog ←or→ a cat in your next life?

1387. Pencil ←or→ ink?

1388. Get married in your dream location ←or→ on your dream date?

1389. Live by a park ←or→ live by the beach?

1390. Be made out of sand ←or→ made out of salt?

1391. Be able to set fires with your mind ←or→ move objects with your mind?

1392. Have snakes for hair ←or→ wheels for feet?

1393. Be able to lift tons ←or→ run a fast mile?

1394. Have bare walls ←or→ have your walls completely covered with posters?

1395. Have a famous portrait ←or→ pose for your own?

1396. Be an executive assistant ←or→ a mid-level employee with no assistant?

1397. Star on a hit show for one season ←or→ an okay show for 10 seasons?

1398. Have a designated parking spot everywhere you go ←or→ a have a driver pick you up and drop you off?

1399. Have dinner in Spain ←or→ dessert in Italy?

1400. Walk everywhere in France ←or→ drive everywhere in Ireland?

1401. Go on a guided tour ←or→ sightsee on your own?

1402. Go to a gift shop ←or→ a stationary shop?

1403. Reread your favorite book 20 times ←or→ read 20 new books?

1404. Worry for nothing ←or→ never worry but get blindsided?

1405. Plan for the future ←or→ dwell on the past?

1406. Do meditation ←or→ physical exercises?

1407. Word games ←or→ board games?

1408. Read only books you hate ←or→ never read again?

1409. Be a bookworm ←or→ an earthworm?

1410. Encounter the Loch Ness monster ←or→ Bigfoot?

1411. See a rainbow ←or→ a shooting star?

1412. Be a leprechaun ←or→ a cherub?

1413. Be stressed ←or→ be sick?

1414. Be funny ←or→ charming?

1415. Marry a monarch ←or→ your soulmate?

1416. Be royalty ←or→ a famous actor?

1417. Run a government ←or→ a successful business?

1418. A medieval torch ←or→ a lantern?

1419. Lose power ←or→ lose your phone?

1420. Have a refrigerator that never runs out of food ←or→ a dresser that never runs out of clothes?

1421. Sleep with the lights on ←or→ work with the lights off?

1422. Nap in a hammock ←or→ on the couch?

1423. Give everything up for a loved one ←or→ give up a loved one?

1424. Ear infection ←or→ a throat infection?

1425. Carsick ←or→ seasick?

1426. Giggle ←or→ guffaw?

1427. Loud sneeze ←or→ quiet sneeze?

1428. Coughing cold ←or→ sneezing cold?

1429. Bite your tongue ←or→ bite your cheek?

1430. Have chapped lips ←or→ chapped hands?

1431. Cactus ←or→ fresh flowers?

1432. Collect pinecones ←or→ acorns?

1433. Have a self-driving car ←or→ a self-cleaning house?

1434. Have a pet hamster ←or→ a pet gerbil?

1435. Own a theme park ←or→ own a circus?

1436. Be a dog catcher ←or→ a lion tamer?

1437. Have carrots and hummus ←or→ celery and peanut butter?

1438. Cheese fondue ←or→ chocolate fondue?

1439. Big family reunion ←or→ small family holiday party?

1440. Celebrate the new year ←or→ your birthday?

1441. Have a birthday party in Paris ←or→ a bachelor party in Rome?

1442. Take a deep breath ←or→ let out a loud scream?

1443. Write run-on sentences ←or→ get to the point?

1444. Have too much work and not enough time ←or→
too much time and not enough work?

1445. Write for a famous newspaper ←or→ a famous news program?

1446. Write for a magazine publisher ←or→ a book publisher?

1447. Ride in a hot air balloon ←or→ a blimp?

1448. Dry skin ←or→ oily skin?

1449. Read for four hours ←or→ run for one hour?

1450. Eat an entire pizza in 10 minutes ←or→ five hamburgers in an hour?

1451. Have a car with cruise control ←or→ heated seats?

1452. Blow up a house ←or→ crash a car?

1453. Have candy for breakfast ←or→ cookies for dinner?

1454. Ride a horse ←or→ a motorcycle?

1455. Be a spy ←or→ an assassin?

1456. Be an architect ←or→ an engineer?

1457. Design houses ←or→ build houses?

1458. Be an alpha wolf ←or→ a lone wolf?

1459. Give love ←or→ be loved?

1460. Give a lot to charity but no one knows ←or→ give a little to charity but everyone knows?

1461. Instant photos ←or→ instant noodles?

1462. Fizzy water ←or→ still water?

1463. Fizzy water ←or→ soda?

1464. Organic meat ←or→ non-organic vegetables?

1465. Miss your BFF ←or→ miss your crush?

1466. Have a long-distance relationship with your soul mate ←or→ a local relationship with someone you only sort of like?

1467. Layflat notebook ←or→ spiral bound notepad?

1468. Black ink ←or→ blue ink?

1469. Gel pens ←or→ felt pens?

1470. Tape measure ←or→ ruler?

1471. Staples ←or→ tape?

1472. Run in a field of flowers ←or→ climb an oak tree?

1473. Pine ←or→ maple?

1474. Raven ←or→ hawk?

1475. Butterflies ←or→ moths?

1476. Get lost at sea ←or→ lost in the desert?

1477. Get pricked by a cactus ←or→ stung by a bee?

1478. Float in the water ←or→ float amongst the clouds?

1479. Be a strict mom ←or→ a cool mom?

1480. Fig cookies ←or→ chocolate chip cookies?

1481. Tex Mex ←or→ authentic Mexican food?

1482. Walk a runway ←or→ run a marathon?

1483. Be an investment banker ←or→ invest in banks?

1484. Bagel with cream cheese ←or→ bagel with butter?

1485. Backache ←or→ a stomachache?

1486. Drive-thru ←or→ pick up?

1487. Collect rare stamps ←or→ rare collect postcards?

1488. English muffin ←or→ toast?

1489. Burn your hand ←or→ burn your tongue?

1490. Read your diary to your crush ←or→ to your mom?

1491. Have five-day weekends ←or→ five-hour workdays?

1492. Pigtails ←or→ manbun?

1493. Hike up a mountain ←or→ hike through the jungle?

1494. Catch the biggest fish of your life but have to throw it back ←or→ catch average-sized fish but get to keep them all?

1495. Unlimited lobster ←or→ unlimited crab legs?

1496. Dictionary ←or→ thesaurus?

1497. Swim through a swamp ←or→ get stuck in quicksand?

1498. Swim with a mermaid ←or→ ride a unicorn?

1499. Live in a messy house cluttered with beautiful objects ←or→ a neat house that only contains the bare necessities?

1500. Have the world's longest nose hair ←or→ the world's longest ear hair?

1501. Have the world longest eyebrows ←or→ the world's longest eyelashes?

1502. Have to wear a full face of makeup every day ←or→ heavy gold jewelry every day?

1503. Work at a toy store ←or→ a candy store?

1504. Meet one of your ancestors ←or→ one of your descendants?

1505. Snorkel ←or→ water ski?

1506. Black beans ←or→ kidney beans?

1507. Strawberries ←or→ blueberries?

1508. Raspberries ←or→ blackberries?

1509. Wear a crown everywhere ←or→ a cape everywhere?

1510. Live in a tree house ←or→ an igloo?

1511. Have a horse ←or→ a llama?

1512. Pretzels ←or→ potato chips?

1513. Drink everything from a baby bottle ←or→ from a sippy cup?

1514. Drink a glass of maple syrup ←or→ a glass of tomato sauce?

1515. Live in a house with no windows ←or→
a house with huge windows but no curtains?

1516. Have a pet tarantula ←or→ pet snake?

1517. Be a firefly ←or→ a butterfly?

1518. Eat a whole jalapeño ←or→ a whole lemon?

1519. Pumpkin pie ←or→ sweet potato pie?

1520. Have to see someone you hate every day ←or→ only get to see someone you love once a year?

1521. Be a famous athlete ←or→ a famous singer?

1522. Do yoga ←or→ dance?

1523. Play drums ←or→ bass?

1524. Knit ←or→ sew?

1525. Be a novelist ←or→ a painter?

1526. Publish one great novel ←or→ 30 mediocre ones?

1527. Marry your worst enemy ←or→ a complete stranger?

1528. Sleep in jeans every night ←or→ wear pajama pants in public every day?

1529. Never buy new clothes again ←or→ never buy new shoes again?

1530. Work somewhere where you have a mean boss but nice coworkers ←or→ somewhere where you have a nice boss but mean coworkers?

1531. Eat a live worm ←or→ a dead cockroach?

1532. Give up bread ←or→ cake?

1533. Not eat for a day ←or→ not drink any liquid for a day?

1534. Decaf coffee ←or→ herbal tea?

1535. Give up bread ←or→ meat?

1536. Eat raw ←or→ cooked carrots?

1537. Muffins ←or→ donuts?

1538. Eat an entire tub of frosting plain ←or→
eat an entire cake with no frosting on it?

1539. Drink a protein shake ←or→ a smoothie?

1540. Make s'mores with charred marshmallows ←or→
untoasted marshmallows?

1541. Be a DJ ←or→ a rapper?

1542. Be a singer ←or→ a producer?

1543. Be a pop star ←or→ a Broadway star?

1544. Sleep with a creepy doll in your room ←or→
constantly wear a supposedly cursed necklace?

1545. Never brush your hair again ←or→ never brush your teeth again?

1546. Wear the logo of a band you hate ←or→ sports team you hate?

1547. Be able to move things with your mind ←or→ see the future?

1548. Have a three-year-old chose your outfit every day ←or→ have to wear a
different Halloween costume every day?

1549. Listen to the best song on your least favorite album ←or→ the worst song on your favorite album?

1550. Be able to change your hair color at will ←or→ the length of your hair at will?

1551. Never eat fruit again ←or→ never eat vegetables again?

1552. Be an acrobat ←or→ be a contortionist?

1553. Live inside a musical ←or→ inside a cartoon?

1554. Have the same first and last name as a celebrity ←or→ as your best friend?

1555. Wear a fedora ←or→ a feather boa?

1556. Talk in your sleep ←or→ walk in your sleep?

1557. Write songs ←or→ poetry?

1558. Be a lyricist ←or→ composer?

1559. Be a cowboy ←or→ a pirate?

1560. Get sunburned ←or→ caught in the rain?

1561. Be a biologist ←or→ a physicist?

1562. Have a big dog ←or→ a small dog?

1563. Have an aquarium ←or→ houseplants?

1564. Write a short story ←or→ a novel?

1565. Write a children's book ←or→ an adult book?

1566. Write a mystery novel ←or→ a romance novel?

1567. Have your teacher walk in on you on the toilet ←or→
your crush walk in on you in the shower?

1568. Eat something that looks disgusting but tastes great ←or→
looks great but tastes disgusting?

1569. Have a pit bull ←or→ a poodle?

1570. Rice ←or→ pasta?

1571. Take an eight-hour bus ride with your nosy aunt ←or→ your annoying ex?

1572. Raise chickens ←or→ goats?

1573. Sudoku ←or→ a crossword puzzle?

1574. Learn to knit ←or→ cook?

1575. Paint something abstract ←or→ paint something realistic?

1576. Wear your jeans backwards ←or→ your shoes on the wrong feet?

1577. Dog shows ←or→ cooking shows?

1578. Only be able to communicate with your friends by talking on phone ←or→
never be able to talk to them on the phone again?

1579. Leave your Christmas decorations up all year long ←or→ have to put up elaborate decorations for every holiday, no matter how minor?

1580. Wait in line for a bathroom during a parade ←or→ in a stadium during a sporting event?

1581. Go bowling ←or→ go to an arcade?

1582. Play air hockey ←or→ real hockey?

1583. Ice fish ←or→ ice skate?

1584. Have your backyard infested by crows ←or→ by squirrels?

1585. Play tetherball ←or→ foursquare?

1586. Have a movie marathon ←or→ binge watch a TV show?

1587. Read the entire dictionary ←or→ wait in line to get your driver's license?

1588. Have your boss see you sing karaoke ←or→ see you in footie pajamas?

1589. Have your crush see you sing karaoke ←or→ see you in footie pajamas?

1590. Have a boss who doesn't know what they're doing but gives you independence ←or→ a competent boss who is a micromanager?

1591. Wear a sweater in the summer ←or→ shorts in the winter?

1592. Never wear clothing with pockets again ←or→ never carry a bag again?

1593. Only be able to eat pureed food for the rest of your life ←or→ only be able to eat food that is white for the rest of your life?

1594. Be terrible at cooking ←or→ terrible at driving?

1595. Be clumsy ←or→ messy?

1596. Spend seven hours on a plane ←or→ seven hours in a car?

1597. Raise chickens ←or→ bees?

1598. Pole dance ←or→ belly dance?

1599. Boxing ←or→ MMA?

1600. Live in the countryside ←or→ city?

1601. Only be able to read children's' books for the rest of your life ←or→ only be able to read cheesy romance novels for the rest of your life?

1602. Invent something that changes the world ←or→ something that makes you rich?

1603. Make a scientific discovery that saves lives ←or→ be the world's most generous philanthropist?

1604. Invent something that changes the world ←or→ be the leader of a country?

1605. Only wear black for a year ←or→ have to have braces for a year?

1606. Sleep on the top bunk ←or→ bottom bunk?

1607. Be on a plane ride with a barking dog ←or→ a crying baby?

1608. Have to wear a tutu to work ←or→ have to wear a clown wig to work?

1609. Give up candy ←or→ coffee?

1610. Accidentally insult a relative ←or→
accidentally break a precious family heirloom?

1611. Be thrown a surprise party ←or→ throw someone else a surprise party?

1612. Carry rocks in your pockets at all times ←or→
have a rock in your shoe at all times?

1613. Work from home but have to cook all your own meals ←or→
work in an office with free meals in a fancy cafeteria?

1614. Work 12-hour days with a 15-minute commute ←or→
6-hour days with a 90-minute commute?

1615. Raise funds via a car wash ←or→ a bake sale?

1616. Baked bacon ←or→ sautéed sausage?

1617. Drink a bottle of mouthwash ←or→ eat a tube of toothpaste?

1618. Miss Halloween ←or→ your birthday?

1619. Have to floss three times a day ←or→ brush your hair three times a day?

1620. Volunteer at a pet shelter ←or→ a library?

1621. Fly economy to the destination of your dreams ←or→ fly first class to a destination that is just okay?

1622. Build a bookcase ←or→ paint a room?

1623. Bake your best friend a birthday cake that is beautiful but tastes bad ←or→ is ugly but tastes delicious?

1624. Have a haircut that you love but everyone you know makes fun of ←or→ have a haircut that you hate but everyone you know constantly compliments?

1625. Wear clothes that are too tight all day ←or→ clothes that are slightly damp all day?

1626. Collect gemstones ←or→ seashells?

1627. Be able to touch the tip of your nose with your tongue ←or→ lick your elbow?

1628. Be forced to stay awake for five nights in a row ←or→ have to sleep on a bed of nails for five nights in a row?

1629. Be a crash test dummy ←or→ have nursing students practice blood draws on you?

1630. Listen to country music ←or→ showtunes?

1631. Go to the opera ←or→ a dance club?

1632. Go to the library ←or→ a concert?

1633. Buy books ←or→ check them out from the library?

1634. Give up eating your favorite food ←or→ listening to your favorite musical artist?

1635. Lend your friend your favorite shirt and they forget to return it ←or→ lend your friend your favorite shirt and they return it torn?

1636. Have a flower garden ←or→ a vegetable garden?

1637. Meet a phoenix ←or→ a dragon?

1638. Not have a car ←or→ not have a computer?

1639. Be able to turn invisible ←or→ be able to grow ←or→ shrink at will?

1640. Watch the news on TV ←or→ read a newspaper?

1641. Swim for an hour every day for a year ←or→ run for an hour every day for a year?

1642. Read a novel ←or→ a nonfiction book?

1643. Read a magazine ←or→ a newspaper?

1644. Read an e-book ←or→ a physical book?

1645. Grow sunflowers ←or→ roses?

1646. Have an apple tree ←or→ a berry bush in your yard?

1647. Be able to communicate with birds ←or→ fish?

1648. Have a taco truck ←or→ an ice cream truck parked on your street?

1649. Tacos ←or→ burritos?

1650. Only be able to eat with just your hands for the rest of your life ←or→ be able to eat with utensils but only directly off of the table?

1651. Not be able to travel outside of your town for a year ←or→ not celebrate any holidays for a year?

1652. Eat your least favorite dessert ←or→ your favorite vegetable?

1653. Eat pizza ←or→ brownies for breakfast?

1654. Wear glasses ←or→ braces?

1655. Binge watch your favorite TV show ←or→ go to an amusement park?

1656. Never get to read the last book in your favorite series ←or→ never see the season finale of your favorite TV show?

1657. Have a costume party wedding ←or→ a wedding on a boat?

1658. Have a wedding on a tropical island ←or→ a wedding in your backyard?

1659. Eat spaghetti with your fingers ←or→ corn with chopsticks?

1660. Canoe ←or→ kayak?

1661. Ride a horse ←or→ water ski?

1662. Get carsick every time you ride in a car ←or→ get a stomachache every time you eat your favorite food?

1663. Get motion sickness on boats ←or→ planes?

1664. Eat a donut ←or→ a bagel?

1665. Eat toast ←or→ cereal?

1666. Watch a TV show ←or→ listen to a podcast?

1667. Be stuck on a desert island with a group of beauty pageant contestants ←or→ a group of reality TV stars?

1668. Stream your favorite album but have to listen to advertisements every third song ←or→ stream an album you don't particularly like but with no ads?

1669. Watch your favorite TV show with ads ←or→ a TV show you only sort of like but with no ads?

1670. Have a tree growing inside your house ←or→ a koi pond inside your house?

1671. Have a live-in cleaning staff so that you never have to do chores but also get no privacy ←or→ live in privacy but have to do all your own chores?

1672. Vacuum ←or→ dust?

1673. Work at a fast food restaurant ←or→ a grocery store?

1674. Work at a bookstore ←or→ a flower shop?

1675. Have an in-home gym ←or→ an in-home movie theater?

1676. Be able to use only ketchup ←or→ only mustard for the rest of your life?

1677. Have a pet parrot ←or→ a pet chinchilla?

1678. Have a rabbit ←or→ a guinea pig?

1679. Clean a hamster cage ←or→ a fish tank?

1680. Pet sit ←or→ babysit?

1681. Pet sit ←or→ house sit?

1682. Be a tutor ←or→ a nanny?

1683. Be a doctor ←or→ a lawyer?

1684. Play your favorite board game with people you hate ←or→ your least favorite board game with your best friends?

1685. Write 20 long and detailed thank you notes for birthday gifts you received ←or→ don't receive any birthday gifts at all?

1686. Receive 10 birthday gifts that you don't like ←or→ no birthday gifts at all?

1687. Receive one big gift ←or→ 10 small gifts?

1688. Shop at a thrift store ←or→ in the clearance section of a department store?

1689. Wear only camo print for the rest of your life ←or→ only neon colors for the rest of your life?

1690. Throw up one time every day ←or→ pee your pants one time every day?

1691. Pee yourself in public once a week ←or→
poop yourself in public once a year?

1692. Eat earthworms covered in tomato sauce ←or→
spaghetti noodles covered in mud?

1693. Soup ←or→ salad?

1694. Fruit salad ←or→ veggie salad?

1695. Iceberg lettuce ←or→ spinach?

1696. Be a massive one-hit wonder and then fade into obscurity ←or→
be moderately famous for your whole life?

1697. Melt when water touches you ←or→ burst into flames in direct sunlight?

1698. Wear socks with holes ←or→ have a pebble in your shoe?

1699. Go a week without changing your underwear ←or→
go a week without changing your socks?

1700. Wear a top hat every day ←or→ a cowboy hat every day?

1701. Sunburn super easily ←or→ have sensitive skin that gets a rash from
most soaps and lotions?

1702. Have to wear a metal crown everywhere ←or→
a splintering wooden crown everywhere?

1703. Be sent to jail for a year for a crime but your family and friends all think you are innocent ←or→ be acquitted but your family and friends all think you are guilty?

1704. Wear dangle earrings ←or→ studs?

1705. Eat salad without dressing ←or→ a hamburger without condiments?

1706. Live in the same place for the rest of your life ←or→ have to move somewhere new every year for the rest of your life?

1707. Have bird wings ←or→ butterfly wings?

1708. Have dragon wings ←or→ dragonfly wings?

1709. Have sharp claws ←or→ a poison bite?

1710. Chocolate ←or→ caramel?

1711. Licorice ←or→ gummy candy?

1712. Have two small horns on the top of your head ←or→ one big horn sticking out of your forehead?

1713. Have green skin ←or→ antennae?

1714. Eat food off the ground outside ←or→ the floor of your kitchen?

1715. Play harmonica ←or→ accordion?

1716. Be able to control the weather ←or→ control time?

1717. Be able to transform into a shark ←or→ a tiger?

1718. Have perfect skin and greasy hair ←or→ greasy skin and perfect hair?

1719. Have dry skin ←or→ dandruff?

1720. Use only shampoo for the rest of your life ←or→
only conditioner for the rest of your life?

1721. Wash your hands with only hot sauce ←or→ melted cheese?

1722. Instantly end all poverty ←or→ all disease?

1723. Be a poor political leader ←or→ a wealthy private citizen?

1724. Have no roof ←or→ no locking doors in your home?

1725. Do yoga ←or→ meditate?

1726. Be able to speak all human languages ←or→
communicate with all animals?

1727. Only see ghosts ←or→ only hear ghosts?

1728. Be a doctor on a medical drama ←or→ a detective on a crime drama?

1729. Wear only mascara every day ←or→ only lipstick every day?

1730. Eat a spoonful of cinnamon ←or→ an entire tub of ice cream?

1731. Play the hero in a small indie film ←or→ the villain in a huge blockbuster?

1732. Be named after your parents' favorite food ←or→ favorite city?

1733. Be named after your parents' favorite flower ←or→ favorite gemstone?

1734. Color with crayons ←or→ finger paint?

1735. Use oil pastels ←or→ chalk pastels?

1736. Use watercolors ←or→ acrylic paint?

1737. Pop a pimple ←or→ leave it alone?

1738. Blackheads ←or→ whiteheads?

1739. Be in charge of a small country ←or→
the second-in-command for a huge one?

1740. Have the head of a bull ←or→ a snake tail instead of legs?

1741. Work in a bakery ←or→ a candy factory?

1742. Be a well-known politician who is really just a figurehead ←or→
an unknown one who pulls the strings behind the scenes?

1743. Play flute ←or→ violin?

1744. Play guitar ←or→ piano?

1745. Play guitar ←or→ ukulele?

1746. Eat an unfamiliar mushroom in the woods ←or→ an unfamiliar berry?

1747. Be punished for a murder but have a clear conscience ←or→
away with a murder but have it weigh on your conscience forever?

1748. Have to talk to your enemy every day ←or→
only be able to talk to your best friend once a month?

1749. Wear clown makeup everywhere for a week ←or→
have a face tattoo for the rest of your life?

1750. Broccoli ←or→ brussels sprouts?

1751. Broccoli ←or→ asparagus?

1752. See the future in tea leaves ←or→ a crystal ball?

1753. Have a bad back ←or→ bad knees?

1754. Be lactose intolerant ←or→ get headaches from caffeine?

1755. Have fingers for toes ←or→ toes for fingers?

1756. Go to kindergarten again for a year ←or→
be a kindergarten teacher for a year?

1757. Wear a backpack that isn't big enough to hold all of your things ←or→
a backpack that is massive and heavy?

1758. Messenger bag ←or→ a briefcase?

1759. Fast food ←or→ homemade?

1760. Lunchbox ←or→ a paper bag?

1761. Watch the first act of a play you love but not being able to return after intermission ←or→ be forced to sit through the entirety of a three hour play you hate?

1762. Eat a spoon of raw sugar every day for the rest of your life ←or→ never be able to eat dessert again?

1763. Make potions ←or→ cast spells with a wand?

1764. Work in a frosting factory ←or→ a sprinkle factory?

1765. Shop in a thrift store ←or→ an expensive boutique?

1766. Be caught in a huge lie by your enemy ←or→ lie hugely to someone you love and get away with it?

1767. Trip in public ←or→ fart in public?

1768. Get free music for life ←or→ free television streaming for life?

1769. Bake a cake ←or→ plant a garden?

1770. Knit a scarf ←or→ build a table?

1771. Live in a wooden house ←or→ a brick house?

1772. Be called an embarrassing but endearing nickname by your family every time you are in public together ←or→ be called a cruel nickname by a stranger?

1773. Own expensive jewelry ←or→ an expensive car?

1774. Drive a convertible ←or→ an old-school hippie van?

1775. Be overdressed ←or→ underdressed for every occasion?

1776. Have to wear pajamas every day for the rest of your life ←or→
a suit every day for the rest of your life?

1777. Wear a wedding dress to someone else's wedding ←or→
a brightly colored Hawaiian shirt to a funeral?

1778. Sew all your own clothes ←or→ cook all your own food from scratch?

1779. Have to exercise every day ←or→ only be able to exercise once a year?

1780. Be insulted in a deeply personal way by a stranger ←or→ in a broad way
by a friend?

1781. Peppermint ←or→ toffee?

1782. Donuts with ←or→ without frosting?

1783. Jelly-filled donuts ←or→ cream-filled donuts?

1784. Get a rash from touching your pet ←or→
a rash from eating your favorite food?

1785. Always carry all your belongings in a wicker basket ←or→
in a plastic bucket?

1786. Own all wicker furniture ←or→ furniture that is of any material that you
want but always has to have a clear plastic sheet over it?

1787. Only sit in rocking chairs ←or→ only sit on stools?

1788. Only sit in papasans ←or→ only sit in swivel chairs?

1789. Iced tea ←or→ hot tea?

1790. Sparkling water ←or→ lemon water?

1791. Only be able to get your news from a news source that is biased towards your views ←or→ a news source that is biased against your views?

1792. Be a clown ←or→ a lion tamer?

1793. Be super strong but appear average ←or→ appear super muscular but really only have average strength?

1794. Have a very small but very neat house ←or→ a very large but very messy house?

1795. Know your success was at someone else's expense ←or→ know that someone else's success was at your expense?

1796. Have a very unusual name ←or→ a very common one?

1797. Know every fact about one famous historical figure ←or→ one fact about every famous historical figure?

1798. Know a lot about a celebrity ←or→ about a famous historical figure?

1799. Go to the beach with no towel ←or→ no sunglasses?

1800. Carry a hairball in your pocket for a day ←or→ in your hand for 10 minutes?

1801. Have to wear polka dots every day for the rest of your life ←or→ stripes every day for the rest of your life?

1802. Discover a dark secret about someone you love ←or→ remain blissfully ignorant?

1803. Eat a rotten apple ←or→ a moldy piece of bread?

1804. Walk a dog ←or→ push a baby in a stroller?

1805. Take a walk in a park carrying a parasol ←or→ wearing a fancy hat?

1806. Get revenge ←or→ take the high road?

1807. Breakfast burrito ←or→ breakfast sandwich?

1808. Scone ←or→ biscuit?

1809. English muffin ←or→ bagel?

1810. Rare steak ←or→ well-done steak?

1811. Have a pet gecko ←or→ a pet iguana?

1812. Be a hermit crab ←or→ be a turtle?

1813. Be a tropical fish ←or→ a sea turtle?

1814. Be a dolphin ←or→ a shark?

1815. Only get to use one emoji in your online communications for the rest of your life ←or→ only get to use one acronym?

1816. Have a lie detector machine evaluating you during a job interview ←or→ a first date?

1817. Walk in on two people making out ←or→ having a heated argument?

1818. Stub your toe ←or→ get a splinter?

1819. Lose sensation in your whole hand for a week ←or→ in one finger forever?

1820. Be paid a lot of money to advertise a brand you hate on your social media ←or→ advertise a brand you love on your social media without being paid?

1821. Listen to a cassette ←or→ a CD?

1822. Ride a tandem bicycle ←or→ a giant tricycle?

1823. Have to translate everything your partner says to everyone else ←or→ have your partner have to translate everything you say to everyone else?

1824. Be a hawk ←or→ an owl?

1825. Be a wolf ←or→ a fox?

1826. Be a hyena ←or→ a coyote?

1827. Be a lion ←or→ a tiger?

1828. Have your footsteps make absolutely no noise whenever you walk ←or→ be able to turn invisible?

1829. Have constant dry throat ←or→ constant watery eyes?

1830. Have a very loud laugh ←or→ a very unusual-sounding laugh?

1831. Pierce your own ears ←or→ give yourself a small tattoo?

1832. Look for a needle in a haystack ←or→
sleep on the haystack without looking for the needle first?

1833. Try to thread a needle in the dark ←or→ with shaky hands?

1834. Creamed corn ←or→ corn on the cob?

1835. Bread pudding ←or→ rice pudding?

1836. Stomped on by an elephant ←or→ crushed by a python?

1837. Be a tree nymph ←or→ a water nymph?

1838. Have an affectionate goldfish ←or→ an indifferent dog?

1839. Be able to make anyone fall in love with you ←or→
make anyone terrified of you?

1840. Attend a party in Marie Antoinette's court ←or→ Cleopatra's?

1841. Always give the perfect gift for every occasion ←or→
always cook the perfect meal?

1842. Always be comfortable making small talk ←or→
always be comfortable having serious conversations?

1843. Be talked to in a baby voice all of the time ←or→
have to talk in a baby voice all of the time?

1844. Be great at archery ←or→ knife-throwing?

1845. Be a great driver who always drives in difficult situations ←or→ a terrible driver who always has a smooth trip?

1846. Be able to win every argument you get into ←or→ be good at keeping calm and avoiding arguments?

1847. Bow tie ←or→ a regular tie?

1848. Be great at cooking meals but terrible at baking ←or→ be great at baking but terrible at cooking meals?

1849. Be okay at cooking everything ←or→ awesome at cooking three things and terrible at cooking everything else?

1850. Give really good compliments ←or→ be a really good listener?

1851. Pool ←or→ darts?

1852. Checkers ←or→ chess?

1853. Card games ←or→ board games?

1854. Snow angels ←or→ snowmen?

1855. Build a snow fort ←or→ have a snowball fight?

1856. Get snow thrown down the back of your neck ←or→ get snow in your shoes?

1857. Always cry silently but end up with a blotchy red face after ←or→ always cry loudly but always look the exact same after as you did before you cried?

1858. Pee in a swimming pool ←or→ a hot tub?

1859. Beach volleyball ←or→ ordinary volleyball?

1860. Take bad advice ←or→ give bad advice to a friend?

1861. Only be able to type in italics for the rest of your life ←or→ only be able to type in bold?

1862. Only be able to type in a funky font for the rest of your life ←or→ only be able to type in a bright color?

1863. Fencing ←or→ taekwondo?

1864. Slide down a rainbow ←or→ sit on a cloud?

1865. Be a hypnotist ←or→ a magician?

1866. Be a terrible cook ←or→ a terrible conversationalist?

1867. Invent a board game ←or→ invent a video game?

1868. Walk into a glass door ←or→ accidentally break a window with a baseball?

1869. Daydream ←or→ nap?

1870. Be the captain of a ship ←or→ the pilot of a plane?

1871. Discover a new planet ←or→ a lost civilization?

1872. Wear awful perfume in public ←or→ smell like body odor in public?

1873. Give up wheat products ←or→ potato products?

1874. Swim with a jellyfish ←or→ a stingray?

1875. Be a sealion ←or→ a seal?

1876. Paper dolls ←or→ origami?

1877. Have a pet squid ←or→ pet octopus?

1878. Have a pet giant panda ←or→ a pet koala?

1879. Never be able to pay for anything in cash ←or→ always have to pay for everything in cash?

1880. Get bitten by a rattlesnake ←or→ stung by a scorpion?

1881. Have to wear ugly Christmas sweaters year-round ←or→ wear a party hat everywhere you go?

1882. Kill a cockroach with your bare hand ←or→ a mouse with your shoe?

1883. Give up hand sanitizer ←or→ lotion?

1884. Give up deodorant ←or→ toothpaste?

1885. Brush your teeth with toothpaste that tastes like dirt for a week ←or→ not brush your teeth for a week?

1886. Read a book that takes place in another country ←or→ on another planet?

1887. Fantasy ←or→ science fiction?

1888. Jump off a high dive ←or→ go down a water slide?

1889. Get a computer virus ←or→ get the flu?

1890. Eat delicious fudge that is so sticky it takes a half hour to chew and swallow ←or→ quickly swallow down soured milk?

1891. Eat an orange peel ←or→ a banana peel?

1892. Cardigan ←or→ pullover sweater?

1893. Sweater ←or→ sweatshirt?

1894. Sandals ←or→ flip flops?

1895. Peanut butter and jelly sandwich ←or→ peanut butter and banana sandwich?

1896. Peanut butter and marshmallow fluff sandwich ←or→ peanut butter and honey sandwich?

1897. Chocolate-covered raisins ←or→ yogurt-covered raisins?

1898. Eat apple sauce ←or→ drink apple juice?

1899. Paint something abstract ←or→ realistic?

1900. Paint a still life ←or→ a portrait?

1901. Have an earache ←or→ a toothache?

1902. Always mispronounce the name of everyone you meet ←or→ always have other people mispronounce your name when they meet you?

1903. Mispronounce every word over five letters ←or→ misspell ever word over five letters?

1904. Always have to hand-wash your clothes ←or→ always have to pay double at every laundromat?

1905. Fly as high as an eagle ←or→ be able to camouflage yourself like a chameleon?

1906. Wear the same color every day for the rest of your life ←or→ the same hairstyle every day for the rest of your life?

1907. Sleep as much as a sloth ←or→ eat as much as a panda?

1908. Glow in the dark ←or→ have skin that turns rainbow whenever you get surprised?

1909. Get a horribly painful shot ←or→ the nasty (but not deadly) illness it prevents?

1910. Have feathers ←or→ scales?

1911. Have horns ←or→ a tail?

1912. Dance ballet ←or→ ballroom?

1913. Tap dance ←or→ Irish dance?

1914. Be beautiful but socially awkward ←or→ ugly but with great social skills?

1915. Have a blister ←or→ a stubbed toe?

1916. Wear hair extensions ←or→ false eyelashes?

1917. Explore a newly discovered landmass ←or→ take a vacation to any city of your choice?

1918. Own a library of books that all have the same cover so you can't tell them apart without looking inside ←or→ have a library of books that are old and starting to fall apart?

1919. Wear colored contact lenses ←or→ artificial nails?

1920. Own a gorgeous grand piano but be mediocre at playing it ←or→ own a tiny, run-down keyboard but be amazing at playing it?

1921. Play the bagpipes ←or→ the tuba?

1922. Play the tambourine ←or→ the triangle?

1923. Only be able to eat off fine china ←or→ only be able to eat off paper plates?

1924. Dress in a steampunk style ←or→ a goth style?

1925. Wear glittery shoes ←or→ shoes with soles that light up when you walk?

1926. Automatically be excellent at every sport you try to play ←or→ every instrument you try to play?

1927. Be a lonely genius ←or→ a person of average intelligence with many friends?

1928. Wear your pants backwards all day without noticing ←or→ your shirt inside-out all day without noticing?

1929. Have crumbs on your face all day without noticing ←or→ a food stain on your shirt all day without noticing?

1930. Be in deep unrequited love with one person ←or→ have a new unrequited crush on someone every week?

1931. Do incredibly accurate impressions ←or→ draw hilarious caricatures?

1932. Be able to imitate anyone's singing voice ←or→ anyone's speaking voice?

1933. Get advice from your best friend ←or→ your parent?

1934. Go dancing ←or→ go to the movies?

1935. See a new movie you've never seen before ←or→ watch an old favorite?

1936. Have a flight delayed by 24 hours ←or→ lose all your luggage?

1937. Sing everything you say for the rest of your life ←or→ never sing again for the rest of your life?

1938. Pay double for a flight ←or→ lose all your luggage?

1939. Wear sweatpants to your own wedding ←or→ rip your dress/tuxedo?

1940. Have to wear 1950s-style clothing every day ←or→ have to wear-1980s-style clothing for a day?

1941. Have to wear 1990s-style clothing every day ←or→ 2000s-style clothing every day?

1942. Fuzzy socks ←or→ socks with a pattern?

1943. Bows ←or→ flowers in your hair?

1944. Sherbet ←or→ sorbet?

1945. Chicken nuggets ←or→ fried chicken on the bone?

1946. Baked potato ←or→ mashed potatoes?

1947. Macaroni and cheese ←or→ cheese fries?

1948. Macaroni and cheese with bacon ←or→ with jalapeno peppers?

1949. Wake up early to make sure you're on time ←or→ sleep in and risk running late?

1950. Have your clothes catch on fire ←or→ your hair catch on fire?

1951. Spend a day with ketchup on your face ←or→ spinach in your teeth?

1952. Have 24 hours of sunlight ←or→ 24 hours of darkness?

1953. Live alone in a huge mansion ←or→ with someone you love in a shack?

1954. Be great at your job but none of your coworkers like you ←or→ terrible at your job but all of your coworkers like you?

1955. Skydive ←or→ ride in a hot air balloon?

1956. Hang glide ←or→ zip line?

1957. Hunt for meat ←or→ forage for nuts and fruits?

1958. Eat stinky cheese ←or→ drink black coffee?

1959. Loofah ←or→ washcloth?

1960. Have wrinkles ←or→ gray hair at age 17?

1961. Live in ancient Greece ←or→ ancient Egypt?

1962. Have an ant colony ←or→ a spider's nest in your bedroom?

1963. Have a bird's nest ←or→ a beehive in your bedroom?

1964. Have a monster under your bed ←or→ in your closet?

1965. Be a monster that lives under a bed ←or→ in a closet?

1966. Have a star ←or→ a galaxy named after you?

1967. Have a country ←or→ a planet named after you?

1968. Have your favorite author write your biography ←or→ your favorite actor play you in a movie about your life?

1969. Have gray ←or→ white hair?

1970. Egg rolls ←or→ dumplings?

1971. Daisies ←or→ tulips?

1972. Be caught in a storm with thunder but no lightning ←or→ lightning but no thunder?

1973. Toast with jam ←or→ butter?

1974. Break a rib ←or→ knock an adult tooth out?

1975. Have lint ←or→ pet hair on your clothes?

1976. Have lint ←or→ pet hair on your furniture?

1977. Croissant ←or→ a crêpe?

1978. Cheat off your crush's test and get a perfect score but they saw you do it ←or→ cheat off your crush's test and get a bad score but they didn't see you?

1979. Take care of one elephant ←or→ 200 mice?

1980. Write in bubble letters ←or→ block letters?

1981. Chew mint-flavored gum ←or→ fruity gum?

1982. Chew bubble gum ←or→ cinnamon gum?

1983. Stay in a fancy hotel ←or→ a hotel with a unique theme?

1984. Stay in a medieval-themed hotel ←or→ a space-themed hotel?

1985. Stay in a clown-themed hotel ←or→ a doll-themed hotel?

1986. Brush your hair ←or→ comb your hair?

1987. Only be able to clean your teeth by brushing them ←or→ by flossing them?

1988. Only be able to clean your teeth by flossing ←or→ by mouthwash?

1989. Analog clock ←or→ a digital one?

1990. Motorized wheelchair ←or→ walker?

1991. Fangs ←or→ claws?

1992. Be a hideous monster with a good heart ←or→ a good-looking but evil siren?

1993. Be an evil queen ←or→ a wicked witch?

1994. Start your own country ←or→ be the leader of the country you live in?

1995. Have bubbles come out of your mouth every time you talk ←or→ cry tears made of soda?

1996. Have an overbite ←or→ an underbite?

1997. Wear headgear 24/7 for a year ←or→ braces for three years?

1998. Have a huge gap between your front teeth ←or→ be missing a back tooth?

1999. Have constant bad breath ←or→ be missing several teeth?

2000. Have very crooked teeth ←or→ very yellow teeth?

2001. Barrettes ←or→ a headband?

2002. Buns ←or→ ponytails?

2003. Whipped cream ←or→ chocolate pudding?

2004. Yogurt ←or→ smoothies?

2005. Eat soggy cereal ←or→ dry cereal with no milk?

2006. Eat cereal in orange juice ←or→ cereal in water?

2007. Eat a glazed donut ←or→ a powdered sugar donut?

2008. Take boring classes at a prestigious university ←or→ fascinating classes at a university with a poor reputation?

2009. Sleep in grass ←or→ on a hardwood floor?

2010. Shower in freezing cold water ←or→ shower without a towel to dry off with afterwards?

2011. Copper ←or→ bronze?

2012. Be unlucky in love ←or→ bad at making friends?

2013. Be as small as a thimble ←or→ as large as a skyscraper?

2014. Cut your hair with a knife ←or→ trim your nails with scissors?

2015. Have a pet dinosaur ←or→ a pet dragon?

2016. Have a bucket of glitter dumped on you ←or→ a bucket of paint?

2017. Have constantly bad breath ←or→ constantly matted hair?

2018. Pom-poms ←or→ googly eyes?

2019. Pipe cleaners ←or→ modelling clay?

2020. Blow glass ←or→ make clay pottery?

2021. Be a masseuse ←or→ a pedicurist?

2022. Make jewelry ←or→ do nail art?

2023. Paint a huge mural on a wall ←or→ a tiny portrait on a brooch?

2024. Anklet ←or→ toe ring?

2025. Mood ring ←or→ lava lamp?

2026. Play a video game in an arcade ←or→ in your house?

2027. Watch a movie in a theater ←or→ in your house?

2028. Know one magic trick that fools 100% of people who witness it ←or→ 10 magic tricks that fool 50% of people who witness them?

2029. Have a busted lip ←or→ a cold sore?

2030. Lose a fingernail ←or→ a toenail?

2031. Live with your favorite relative ←or→ your best friend?

2032. Ice cream sundae ←or→ ice cream sandwich?

2033. Bathe in milk ←or→ in an algae-infested pond?

2034. Sweep ←or→ vacuum?

2035. Dust ←or→ wash windows?

2036. Have an embarrassing photo of you posted on social media ←or→ on the bulletin board at your job?

2037. Go to a school for math and science ←or→ a school for the performing arts?

2038. Boarding school ←or→ homeschool?

2039. Sleep-away summer camps ←or→ summer jobs?

2040. Comedy podcasts ←or→ true-crime podcasts?

2041. Live on a street where every house is identical, including your own ←or→ live on a street where every house is identical except yours—and yours is wildly different?

2042. Live in a house painted neon pink ←or→ a house with flowers painted all over the outside?

2043. Live in a ramshackle house in a beautiful neighborhood ←or→ a beautiful house in a run-down neighborhood?

2044. Drive in a fancy car ←or→ live in a fancy house?

2045. Drive in a car that's falling apart ←or→
live in a house that's falling apart?

2046. Jump in a leaf pile ←or→ have a snowball fight?

2047. Ice cream cone ←or→ popsicle?

2048. Picnic ←or→ parade?

2049. Stargaze ←or→ watch a sunset?

2050. Watch a Shakespearean comedy ←or→ tragedy?

2051. Get a bloody nose ←or→ a black eye?

2052. Wear a masquerade mask everywhere ←or→
elbow-length gloves everywhere?

2053. Be able to end all air pollution ←or→ all water pollution?

2054. Be thought of as unintelligent ←or→ unkind?

2055. Be a stand-up comedian ←or→ a satirical writer?

2056. Draw political cartoons ←or→ write op-eds?

2057. Have hair made of spaghetti ←or→ fingernails made of crackers?

2058. Strawberry lemonade ←or→ regular lemonade?

2059. Effortlessly give up any bad habit ←or→ gain any good one?

2060. Be a witch ←or→ a fairy?

2061. Be a mermaid/merman ←or→ a god/goddess?

2062. Be a genie trapped in a bottle ←or→ a prince(ss) trapped in a tower?

2063. Have a massive zit in the middle of your nose ←or→ the middle of your forehead?

2064. Drink terrible-tasting medicine ←or→ get a shot?

2065. Have a name that is very long ←or→ very difficult for others to pronounce?

2066. Open your eyes underwater in a chlorinated swimming pool (with no goggles of course) ←or→ accidentally squirt the juice of an orange into your eye while peeling it?

2067. Have a bucket of salt dumped on you ←or→ a bucket of sugar?

2068. Have a laugh track go off whenever something embarrassing happened to you ←or→ ominous music start to play whenever something bad was about to happen to you?

2069. Be a restaurant critic ←or→ a movie critic?

2070. Be paid to test video games ←or→ candy?

2071. Banana bread ←or→ zucchini bread?

2072. Rigatoni ←or→ penne?

2073. Hot dogs ←or→ bratwurst?

2074. Curly ←or→ straight hair?

2075. Green hair ←or→ blue hair?

2076. Use crystals ←or→ essential oils?

2077. Collect rocks ←or→ plants?

2078. Collect stamps ←or→ foreign currency?

2079. Have pet fish ←or→ pet birds?

2080. Bathe a dog ←or→ clip its nails?

2081. Wear sunglasses at all times ←or→ an eyepatch at all times?

2082. Have super sharp fingernails ←or→ super long fingernails?

2083. Own a vegetable farm ←or→ a fruit orchard?

2084. Take an escalator ←or→ an elevator?

2085. Be a palm tree ←or→ a pine tree?

2086. Use a ride share app ←or→ public transportation?

2087. Bike ←or→ skateboard?

2088. Fight a giant rat ←or→ a giant hornet?

2089. Eat a cake the baker forgot to add sugar to ←or→ a cake where they accidentally added double the amount of sugar needed?

2090. Do ten push-ups ←or→ hold a 1-minute plank?

2091. Candy cane ←or→ round peppermint?

2092. Have a garden full of beautiful weeds ←or→ full of ugly flowers?

2093. Have a front yard with no grass ←or→ a front yard where you can't ever cut the grass?

2094. Live in your car ←or→ in an unused school bus?

2095. Go to a fitness class ←or→ teach a fitness class?

2096. Work at a gym and be paid in free use of the equipment ←or→ work at a spa and be paid in free luxury personal care products?

2097. Go to a personal trainer ←or→ a group fitness class?

2098. Go to a group fitness class with your best friend ←or→ work out just the two of you?

2099. Work out ←or→ get a massage?

2100. Get a massage ←or→ take a bubble bath?

2101. Have a mean guard dog ←or→ a nice dog who's a terrible guard?

2102. Have a small cat ←or→ a big cat?

2103. Have a short-haired dog ←or→ a long-haired dog?

2104. Have a hairless cat ←or→ a long-haired cat?

2105. Have bangs ←or→ a mohawk?

2106. Dye a streak of your hair ←or→ dye just the tips of your hair?

2107. Dye your hair a natural color ←or→ a wild color?

2108. Chemistry ←or→ physics?

2109. Anatomy ←or→ ecology?

2110. Astronomy ←or→ astrology?

2111. Play in a rock band ←or→ an orchestra?

2112. Be in a play ←or→ watch a play?

2113. Design sets ←or→ costumes for a play?

2114. Use a portable cassette player ←or→ CD player?

2115. Green tea ←or→ chai tea?

2116. Be a fashion blogger ←or→ a travel blogger?

2117. Visit a zoo ←or→ an aquarium?

2118. Live in a fish tank ←or→ a hamster cage?

2119. Be somewhere loud ←or→ somewhere quiet?

2120. Be beautiful ←or→ brilliant?

2121. Have to wake up at the exact same time every day ←or→ never be able
to wake up at the same time on different days?

2122. Skip coffee ←or→ skip breakfast?

2123. Smartphone ←or→ a computer?

2124. Laptop ←or→ a tablet?

2125. Be a busboy ←or→ a dishwasher?

2126. Have tattoos completely covering your arms, legs, and torso ←or→
have only one tattoo, but it's on your face?

2127. Let your worst enemy choose an image to get tattooed onto you ←or→
let your most embarrassing relative choose?

2128. Wear sparkly pink earmuffs ←or→ earmuffs decorated with cat ears
on top?

2129. Earmuffs ←or→ a hat?

2130. Go to work in a huge diamond necklace ←or→ a small diamond tiara?

2131. Work on a farm ←or→ in a factory?

2132. Work in silence ←or→ with music?

2133. Get in an argument with your best friend ←or→ your romantic partner?

2134. Use an elliptical ←or→ a stationary bike?

2135. Run on a treadmill ←or→ outdoors?

2136. Be able to run a very long distance, but slowly ←or→ only a very short distance, but extremely fast?

2137. Have a pet hedgehog ←or→ a pet chinchilla?

2138. Stick to a meticulous schedule every day ←or→ wing it?

2139. Cantaloupe ←or→ honeydew melon?

2140. Ping pong ←or→ badminton?

2141. Mango ←or→ kiwi?

2142. Red grapes ←or→ green grapes?

2143. Shave half your head ←or→ your whole head?

2144. Unicycle ←or→ tricycle?

2145. Squats ←or→ lunges?

2146. Give up social media ←or→ movies?

2147. Ruby ←or→ sapphire?

2148. Charm bracelet ←or→ friendship bracelet?

2149. Not show up in mirrors ←or→ not show up on camera?

2150. Not cast a shadow ←or→ not create an echo?

2151. Wear a football uniform—padding and all—everywhere you go for a year ←or→ wear a wetsuit everywhere you go for a year?

2152. Be caught in a thunderstorm ←or→ in hail?

2153. Collect dolls ←or→ stuffed animals?

2154. Wear nothing but a garbage bag for a day ←or→ jump into a full dumpster?

2155. White chocolate ←or→ dark chocolate?

2156. Be an interior designer ←or→ a personal stylist?

2157. Get a free drink with your fast food meal ←or→ a free dessert?

2158. Soft pretzel ←or→ cotton candy?

2159. Give up texting ←or→ email?

2160. Be a gymnast ←or→ a cheerleader?

2161. Go whitewater rafting ←or→ mountain biking?

2162. Be a jockey in a horse race ←or→ drive a racecar?

2163. Parkour ←or→ skateboard?

2164. Scuba dive ←or→ rock climb?

2165. Decorate your walls with paint ←or→ wallpaper?

2166. Have a private swimming pool ←or→ a private sauna?

2167. Have a limousine ←or→ a private jet?

2168. Caramel apple ←or→ a banana split?

2169. Artificial flowers ←or→ real flowers?

2170. Decorate your walls with paintings ←or→ photographs?

2171. Coffee cake ←or→ a cinnamon roll?

2172. Hot chocolate ←or→ hot apple cider?

2173. Have wall-to-wall carpeting that is bright pink ←or→ rainbow polka-dot?

2174. Have a rug that is fluffy ←or→ covered in beautiful patterns?

2175. Paint ←or→ draw?

2176. Be thrill-seeking ←or→ overly cautious?

2177. Swim in the ocean ←or→ read a book on the beach?

2178. Shorts ←or→ pants?

2179. Chocolate cake ←or→ cheesecake?

2180. Rent a house on vacation ←or→ stay in a hotel?

2181. Collect keychains ←or→ refrigerator magnets?

2182. Collect postcards ←or→ snow globes?

2183. Go to a poetry slam ←or→ a concert?

2184. Visit South America ←or→ North America?

2185. Visit ancient ruins ←or→ a modern metropolis?

2186. Visit Europe ←or→ Australia?

2187. Go to an amusement park ←or→ on a cruise?

2188. Wear overalls ←or→ skinny jeans?

2189. Have tile floors in every room of your house ←or→ wall-to-wall carpeting in every room of your house?

2190. Have a home movie theater ←or→ a home arcade?

2191. Listen to music from the 1980s ←or→ the 1990s?

2192. Commission an oil painting of yourself ←or→ of your pet?

2193. Carrot cake ←or→ pumpkin bread?

2194. Cupcakes ←or→ cake pops?

2195. Have a backpack with a cool pattern ←or→ a plain backpack with lots of keychains?

2196. Ride a magic carpet ←or→ climb up a magic beanstalk?

2197. Build a dollhouse ←or→ a treehouse?

2198. Be an elf ←or→ a goblin?

2199. Wear neon green zebra stripes ←or→
hot pink cheetah print every day for the rest of your life?

2200. Have a cellphone with an irritating ringtone ←or→
one that makes no noise when it rings?

2201. Stay up late studying for a test and be tired when you take it ←or→
go to bed early and be well-rested but underprepared when you take it?

2202. Have a constant wedgie ←or→ constantly chafed inner thighs?

2203. Never be able to wear socks again ←or→ always have to wear slippers
instead of real shoes, no matter the weather or occasion?

2204. Wear elbow pads all the time ←or→ knee pads all the time?

2205. Be covered in spikes like a cactus ←or→ leaves like a tree?

2206. Be made of stone ←or→ metal?

2207. Live in a giant bird's nest ←or→ in a cave?

2208. Be able to communicate telepathically with your best friend ←or→
with your pet?

2209. Decorate your house with fairy lights ←or→ paper lanterns?

2210. Eat tree bark ←or→ paper?

2211. Take a walk through autumn leaves ←or→ spring blossoms?

2212. Ravioli ←or→ tortellini?

2213. Be an amazing singer ←or→ amazing at playing an instrument?

2214. Live with a messy roommate ←or→ a loud roommate?

2215. Visit the Bahamas ←or→ Hawaii?

2216. Fall asleep effortlessly every night ←or→
wake up effortlessly every morning?

2217. Cream cheese frosting ←or→ ordinary frosting?

2218. Ice cream cake ←or→ ordinary cake?

2219. Pineapple on pizza ←or→ mushrooms on pizza?

2220. Have a sore neck ←or→ a headache?

2221. Run a marathon while listening to your least favorite song on a constant
loop ←or→ run a marathon while listening to no music at all?

2222. Perfectly remember every image you've ever seen ←or→
every sound you've ever heard?

2223. Have to be on your feet all day at your job ←or→
have to sit at a desk all day?

2224. Be an early bird ←or→ a night owl?

2225. Coffee ←or→ energy drinks?

2226. Go to a club with your parent ←or→ your ex?

2227. Stay up all night ←or→ sleep for 24 hours straight?

2228. Have a rich, grumpy uncle ←or→ a fun, poor uncle?

2229. Write a novel that sells a lot of copies but doesn't win any awards ←or→ a novel that sells poorly but wins many prestigious awards?

2230. Spend a month living on a boat ←or→ spend a month living in a tent?

2231. Have strong opinions that nobody in your life agrees with ←or→ be wishy-washy?

2232. Have a television with a high-quality sound system and low-quality screen ←or→ a low-quality sound system and high-quality screen?

2233. Speak at a commencement ceremony ←or→ give a toast at a wedding?

2234. Be painfully indecisive ←or→ make decisions easily but usually make the wrong decision?

2235. Keep your butter in the fridge ←or→ on the counter?

2236. Blueberry bagels ←or→ cinnamon raisin bagels?

2237. Candy ←or→ raisins?

2238. Cherries ←or→ blueberries?

2239. Chicken fried chicken ←or→ chicken fried steak?

2240. Be an ant ←or→ a spider?

2241. Push the button ←or→ leave it alone?

2242. Take the red pill ←or→ the blue pill?

2243. Wear damp underwear ←or→ damp socks?

2244. Invent the wheel ←or→ sliced bread?

2245. Live without a refrigerator ←or→ a microwave?

2246. Electric stove ←or→ a gas stove?

2247. Give up your washer ←or→ your dryer?

2248. Fight 100 duck sized horses ←or→ one-horse sized duck?

2249. Be stuck on a boat for three weeks ←or→ stuck on a plane?

2250. Have hands for feet ←or→ feet for hands?

2251. Eat food from a trashcan ←or→ starve?

2252. Know the history of everything or every person you come into contact with ←or→ nothing at all?

2253. Time travel ←or→ have super speed?

2254. Be able to eat anything you want ←or→ travel anywhere you want?

2255. Tomato-based pasta sauce ←or→ cream-based pasta sauce?

2256. Watch movies all day ←or→ read/listen to a book?

2257. Be able to know everyone's thoughts ←or→ be invisible?

2258. Be a be world renown stage actor/actress ←or→ a movie star?

2259. Sing opera ←or→ country music?

2260. Be the most powerful person in the world ←or→ the wisest?

2261. Learn to play the guitar ←or→ play the drums?

2262. Be in a rock band ←or→ be in a rap group?

2263. Always be on time ←or→ always be right?

2264. Live in a one level home ←or→ multi-level?

2265. Star in an action movie ←or→ a romantic comedy?

2266. In an apocalypse would you rather be a zombie ←or→ one of the living?

2267. Lose your pinkie toes ←or→ your pinkie fingers?

2268. Learn a foreign language ←or→ a physical activity (i.e. to ski or swim)?

2269. Vacation in the mountains ←or→ at the beach?

2270. Speak only to the living ←or→ the dead?

2271. Be bored all the time ←or→ busy all the time?

2272. Be creative ←or→ successful?

2273. Take a shower ←or→ a bath outdoors?

2274. Use bar soap ←or→ liquid soap?

2275. Be a scientist ←or→ a prolific writer?

2276. Lick a toad ←or→ be licked by a toad?

2277. Cut the grass ←or→ rake leaves?

2278. Eat one food for the rest of your life ←or→
never be able to eat the same food twice for the rest of your life?

2279. Communicate solely via questions ←or→ songs?

2280. Be stranded on a deserted island ←or→ in a jungle?

2281. Win an Emmy ←or→ an Oscar?

2282. Win a Tony ←or→ a Grammy?

2283. Commune with animals ←or→ with the dead?

2284. Move things with your mind ←or→ unlock any door?

2285. Sci-fi horror ←or→ a psychological horror?

2286. Be in a movie ←or→ a music video?

2287. Eat a ghost pepper ←or→ bathe in tomato soup?

2288. Eat a live fish ←or→ curdled milk?

2289. Drink a meal worm milkshake ←or→ a cow liver milkshake?

2290. Have everything you touch turn to candy ←or→ pizza for every meal?

2291. Be in a really good unknown band ←or→ be in a famous band that sucks?

2292. Speak in pig Latin ←or→ Shakespearean English forever?

2293. Be smart with bad luck ←or→ dumb with good luck?

2294. Have teeth made of hard candy ←or→ chocolate?

2295. Have severe frostbite ←or→ third-degree burns?

2296. Be cold ←or→ be hot?

2297. Be lost at sea ←or→ in space?

2298. Grow mushrooms for toes ←or→ branches for fingers?

2299. Give up your phone ←or→ your automobile?

2300. Live in the wilderness ←or→ live in the city?

2301. Sleep on your left side ←or→ on your stomach?

2302. Sleep on your right side ←or→ on your back?

2303. Press rewind ←or→ press fast forward?

2304. Switch lives with a celebrity of your choice only once and die by age 60 ←or→ live as yourself until 150?

2305. Have all the money in the world for the next five years ←or→ live until 90 with an average income?

2306. Live as a creature with gills ←or→ fur?

2307. Have a partner who cheats on you with multiple people in meaningless hookups ←or→ cheated only once but fell in love with that person?

2308. Die by starvation ←or→ drowning?

2309. Die in a fire ←or→ by drowning?

2310. Die by starvation ←or→ by fire?

2311. Be bald ←or→ extremely hairy?

2312. Have eternal youth ←or→ be the smartest person in the world?

2313. Eat anything without gaining weight ←or→ be able to fly?

2314. Racing motorcycle ←or→ cruiser?

2315. Manual ←or→ automatic?

2316. Text ←or→ call?

2317. Never run out of phone battery ←or→ have free Wi-Fi anywhere you go?

2318. Own a teacup pig ←or→ a ferret?

2319. Look strong but be physically weak ←or→ look weak but be physically strong?

2320. Deal with flies ←or→ gnats?

2321. Be with someone who's extremely attractive but has a horrible personality ←or→ be with someone who's unattractive but has the best personality?

2322. Have perfect teeth and horrible breath ←or→ amazing breath and bad teeth?

2323. Be the fastest runner ←or→ the fastest swimmer on Earth?

2324. Plan your life ahead of time ←or→ be spontaneous at all times?

2325. Have hiccups ←or→ stomach rumbles?

2326. Learn to drive a boat ←or→ fly a plane?

2327. Know every song lyric ever written ←or→ know every road and route in the world?

2328. Lose all your possessions and wealth but have love ←or→ lose love but have all your possessions and wealth?

2329. Reward people for being good ←or→ punish people for being bad?

2330. Meet your favorite musical artist ←or→ your favorite actor/actress?

2331. Give up pizza ←or→ pasta?

2332. Always eat cold food ←or→ always drink warm drinks?

2333. Always be right ←or→ always be respected?

2334. Have constant tooth pain ←or→ constant back pain?

2335. Stub a toe ←or→ slam a finger in the door?

2336. Be married ←or→ partners living together?

2337. Get married ←or→ stay single?

2338. Only communicate through hand drawn pictures ←or→ only in yes and no?

2339. Hold a tarantula ←or→ a snake?

2340. Have diarrhea ←or→ constant vomiting?

2341. Be in a world with no laws ←or→ be in a world with too many?

2342. Not have a family ←or→ not have friends?

2343. Be able to speak to all animals ←or→ speak every language?

2344. Always speak your mind even if it hurts people ←or→ never speak again?

2345. Have the ability to be invisible ←or→ to erase memories from your mind?

2346. Have the ability to stop time completely ←or→ rewind it for a do over?

2347. Use only a spoon ←or→ knife for every meal?

2348. Use only a spoon ←or→ fork for every meal?

2349. Use only a fork ←or→ knife for every meal?

2350. Have telekinesis ←or→ mind control?

2351. Eat the same breakfast every morning ←or→ the same dinner every night?

2352. Marry for love ←or→ marry for lots and lots of money?

2353. Have great food ←or→ great sleep?

2354. Drink cow's milk ←or→ goat's milk?

2355. Lose your hearing ←or→ sight?

2356. Date a law student ←or→ a med student?

2357. Be a millionaire ←or→ have inner peace?

2358. Travel the world ←or→ have your dream job?

2359. Master the piano ←or→ the guitar?

2360. Hire a contractor for a home project ←or→ do it yourself?

2361. Be feared by all ←or→ be loved by all?

2362. Spend your money on a cool outfit ←or→ a cool pair of shoes?

2363. Walk into a room to your own theme song ←or→ to a round of applause?

2364. Be somewhere else ←or→ stay where you are forever?

2365. Study in a group ←or→ study on your own?

2366. Remodel your home ←or→ pack up and start somewhere new?

2367. Learn Spanish ←or→ French?

2368. Please others and be at war with yourself ←or→ please yourself and be at war with others?

2369. Have no air conditioner/fan ←or→ no internet?

2370. Eat tacos ←or→ cake for the rest of your life

2371. See the future ←or→ change your past?

2372. Be the king ←or→ the court jester?

2373. Have your camera roll leaked ←or→ your text messages?

2374. Be immortal and never see your family again ←or→
be mortal and have your family in your life?

2375. Be a sports player ←or→ a YouTuber?

2376. Be able to fly for a day ←or→ completely invisible for a day?

2377. Never use social media again ←or→ never watch another movie?

2378. Never watch another TV show ←or→ never use social media again?

2379. Always be surrounded by annoying people ←or→
be alone for the rest of your life?

2380. Die in 50 years with many regrets ←or→ die in 20 years with no regrets?

2381. Be in control ←or→ be brave?

2382. Live by a lake ←or→ by an ocean?

2383. Have a perfect love life ←or→ perfect grades?

2384. American football ←or→ world soccer?

2385. Be in jail/prison for a year ←or→ lose a year of your life?

2386. Always be 10 minutes late ←or→ 20 minutes early?

2387. Know the history of every object you touch ←or→ be able to alter the future?

2388. Be able to talk to land and air animals ←or→ animals that live under water?

2389. Have only green traffic lights on your approach ←or→ never have to stand in line again?

2390. Have three feet ←or→ three hands?

2391. Live without music forever ←or→ without television forever?

2392. Have your dream job ←or→ find your true love?

2393. Have the ability to read people's minds ←or→ make two people fall in love?

2394. Have the same phone forever ←or→ the same haircut forever?

2395. Forget who you are every time it rains ←or→ never be able to remember why you walked into a room?

2396. Lose the ability to speak ←or→ the ability to read?

2397. Sing everything you say ←or→ speak every thought you think?

2398. Know everything and be miserable ←or→ know nothing and be happy?

2399. Have no eyebrows ←or→ just one eyebrow?

2400. Have a weird looking smile ←or→ a weird sounding laugh?

2401. Bathe a dead body ←or→ sleep beside a dead body?

2402. Be buried alive ←or→ be thrown into an evil forest?

2403. Have serial killers as parents ←or→ have your child be a serial killer?

2404. Date someone you love but they don't love you ←or→
date someone who loves you but you don't love them?

2405. Be the funniest person in the room ←or→
the most intelligent with no sense of humor?

2406. Have feet-length arms ←or→ arm-length feet?

2407. Smell like poo all the time and not know it ←or→
be the only one who smells poo everywhere forever?

2408. Be able to play an instrument well ←or→ sing well?

2409. Draw digitally ←or→ draw traditionally?

2410. Know every language ←or→ visit every country?

2411. Be a master magician ←or→ have a superpower?

2412. Read traditionally ←or→ listen to an audiobook?

2413. Be rich ←or→ famous?

2414. Work at a fast food restaurant ←or→ in a coffee shop?

2415. Eat sand ←or→ sunscreen?

2416. Always have a full battery for your phone ←or→
a full tank for your car?

2417. Be able to read minds ←or→ control minds?

2418. Be stranded in a frozen tundra ←or→ in the desert?

2419. Never age physically ←or→ mentally?

2420. Be wealthy in friends ←or→ in cash?

2421. Have a famous life but barely any private time ←or→
have an anonymous life with all the time in the world?

2422. Follow your passion no matter what you may lose ←or→
not lose anything but not follow your passion?

2423. Go to a haunted house ←or→ to a haunted amusement park?

2424. Have your family think the worst of you but have their safety guaranteed
←or→ have your family be in danger but they think good things about you?

2425. Never need or want food again ←or→ never need or
want sleep again?

2426. Be dirt ←or→ trash?

2427. Be the moon ←or→ the sun?

2428. Be a stuffed animal ←or→ a porcelain doll?

2429. Own a mansion ←or→ a tree house in the woods?

2430. Choose a prince charming ←or→ a knight in shining armor?

2431. Eat spicy food ←or→ food with no taste at all?

2432. Travel by hot air balloon ←or→ by chug boat?

2433. Keep your opened ketchup bottle in the fridge ←or→ unrefrigerated in the pantry?

2434. Have a round dining table ←or→ a rectangular one?

2435. Have someone lie to you to make you happy ←or→ someone be honest with you no matter how it may make you feel?

2436. Live in a world of zombies ←or→ in a world of dinosaurs?

2437. Live a life of silence ←or→ blindness if it meant peace in the world?

2438. Find the cure for cancer ←or→ HIV/AIDS?

2439. Party all weekend long ←or→ just stay home?

2440. Have a perfect body ←or→ a perfect face?

2441. Be toned but weigh more because of muscles ←or→
not be toned and weigh less?

2442. Never date and find your soulmate at 70 ←or→ date constantly but
never find "the one" for you?

2443. Live in the same place for the rest of your life ←or→ move every year?

2444. Be a nutritionist ←or→ a therapist?

2445. Wear a meat smelling face mask ←or→
use hand sanitizer that smells like meat?

2446. Never feel another emotion again ←or→ never get sick?

2447. Chinese ←or→ Thai take out/take away?

2448. Be a hero/villain ←or→ the sidekick?

2449. Drink a cup of black coffee ←or→ eat a cup of cookie dough?

2450. Play a game of pure luck ←or→ of pure skill?

2451. Have everything you touch turn to gold ←or→ food?

2452. Get up an hour earlier ←or→ work an hour longer?

2453. Daytime forever ←or→ eternal night?

2454. Be the big spoon ←or→ the little spoon?

2455. Be a fly ←or→ a bee?

2456. Be unable to see color ←or→ unable to taste anything?

2457. Apples ←or→ oranges?

2458. Control the weather ←or→ control minds?

2459. Bring world peace ←or→ end world hunger?

2460. Eat anything without gaining weight ←or→ be able to fly?

2461. Make a popular meme ←or→ become a popular meme?

2462. Have no incisors ←or→ no molars?

2463. Have to always take cold showers ←or→
always get soap in your eyes when showering?

2464. Accidentally have your mic on ←or→ your webcam?

2465. Stub your toe ←or→ step on a sharp toy?

2466. Have the world lose five billion people ←or→
the world lose sixty years of technological progress?

2467. Save your best friend ←or→ your crush?

2468. Eat spiders ←or→ snakes if your life depended on it?

2469. Sleep in a bed full of saw dust ←or→
in one entirely stained with dried blood?

2470. Drink juice with pulp ←or→ juice without pulp?

2471. Eat an entire whole raw fish ←or→
do three months of unpaid plumbing training?

2472. Have a little dog ←or→ a big dog?

2473. Die a hero ←or→ live long enough to become the villain?

2474. Relive your childhood ←or→ win five million dollars?

2475. Eat an onion ←or→ a baseball?

2476. Have a flesh-eating disease for one week that eats away at a body part ←or→ a cold for the rest of your life?

2477. Wear all white all the time ←or→ all black?

2478. Participate in one of the Crusades ←or→ be a Roman gladiator?

2479. Be reliable for everyone and never have time to yourself ←or→ be unreliable and all the time in the world?

2480. Have an insatiable appetite for pizza for the rest of your life ←or→ live on Mars alone for two years?

2481. Walk on a tightrope between two skyscraper buildings ←or→ on a 200-foot ridge?

2482. Live in misery for a year ←or→ fight in a boxing ring every night?

2483. Drive a taxi as a career ←or→ drive a bus?

2484. Be the voice of calm all the time ←or→ be the one to incite turmoil?

2485. Sleep with a bear ←or→ sleep with a mountain lion?

2486. Write job applications for everyone for the next thirty years ←or→
plan banquets?

2487. Be dramatic ←or→ be comedic?

2488. Work a concession stand ←or→ a fast food restaurant?

2489. Sit at a window unable to move ←or→ lay in a bed unable to move?

2490. Go to war for billions of dollars ←or→ maintain peace for one dollar?

2491. Meet an extraterrestrial ←or→ meet a dinosaur?

2492. Break dancing ←or→ line dancing?

2493. Live in a brick house ←or→ a house made of wood?

2494. Be considered mean ←or→ considered nice?

2495. Have your every word be greetings ←or→ uncontrollable laughter?

2496. Play in an orchestra ←or→ on a sports team?

2497. Live in a kitchen ←or→ live in a bathroom?

2498. Have everyone come to you for resolutions to their problems ←or→
live in solitude?

2499. Dig a trench ←or→ dig a hole?

2500. Have to explain why people do the things they do to the person they hurt ←or→ be the one doing the hurting?

2501. Be the dominant force ←or→ the submissive one?

2502. Have only cream in your coffee ←or→ only sugar in your coffee?

2503. Mislead someone to save the life of your pet that makes that person's life worse ←or→ tell the truth and lose your pet making that person's life better?

2504. Be able to ignite fires with your mind ←or→ shoot ice out of your fingertips?

2505. Live on another planet alone ←or→ live on Earth but in a commune?

2506. Tell a lie to benefit you and lose the friendship of your dearest friend ←or→ tell the truth, lose out on your benefit but keep your friend?

2507. Have limited time watching TV ←or→ limited time on social media?

2508. Lead others ←or→ be led?

2509. Deprive yourself of your favorite dessert ←or→ lose both of your pinky toes?

2510. Draw on a blank page ←or→ write on a blank page?

2511. Refer an enemy to get a job you know they'll hate to exact revenge ←or→ give a referral to get a job you know your friend needs to survive?

2512. Drive through fog ←or→ drive through smoke?

2513. Attend school every day nonstop for the next five years ←or→
live on the moon alone with no communication at all for a year.

2514. Share an office space with a colleague who has the flu ←or→
a colleague who has extreme body odor?

2515. Work with metal ←or→ work with wood?

2516. Have everyone consider you an intense person ←or→ consider you a flake?

2517. Have people think you're an absentee friend ←or→
too involved in their lives?

2518. Have prestige ←or→ wealth?

2519. Speak only one dialect and be rich ←or→ multiple and have no money?

2520. Supply the demand ←or→ demand and be supplied?

2521. Always know the way ←or→ always take a chance?

2522. Have an operation to save your eyesight ←or→ your legs?

2523. Drive on a highway ←or→ back roads?

2524. Make a proposal ←or→ accept a proposal?

2525. Have your facial expression always look angry even when you're extremely
happy ←or→ always look happy when you're extremely angry.

2526. Use alcohol on a wound ←or→ peroxide?

2527. Drink green tea ←or→ an avocado smoothie?

2528. Drink a sea of cucumber juice ←or→ a river of asparagus juice?

2529. Lose your sight and never read again ←or→ learn how to read braille?

2530. Lend a book knowing it will never be returned ←or→ lend ten dollars knowing they will never be paid back?

2531. Have a sixth sense ←or→ only four?

2532. Have separation anxiety from your phone ←or→ from your significant other?

2533. Take a shower that's too cold ←or→ a bath that's too hot?

2534. Live behind a fence ←or→ a gate?

2535. Get chills that make your hair stand on end ←or→ a drop in your stomach of impending doom?

2536. Run out of money ←or→ out of Wi-Fi access?

2537. Stay home with a severe flu ←or→ go to work in the best health of your life?

2538. Decorate in bold colors ←or→ pastels?

2539. Come across a leprechaun ←or→ a genie?

2540. Meet a unicorn ←or→ a Pegasus?

2541. Win honestly ←or→ win by cheating?

2542. Hear the sound of fingernails on a chalkboard ←or→ feedback from a microphone and speakers?

2543. Use live worms to fish ←or→ rubber bait?

2544. Speak proper English ←or→ slang all the time?

2545. Understand every piece of artwork created ←or→ be the best singer in the world?

2546. Pay for your lifestyle in hours ←or→ in years?

2547. Have there be something intentional with art work ←or→ there be no meaning at all?

2548. Go into a basement during a horror movie ←or→ go into the attic?

2549. Have ice cream in a cone ←or→ a cup?

2550. Pass up an opportunity of a lifetime if it means making someone else happy ←or→ take the opportunity over someone else's happiness?

2551. Eat a meal without knowing what it actually is ←or→ starve?

2552. Wheat bread ←or→ white?

2553. Clean out a trash can ←or→ clean out a toilet?

2554. Have others made you happy ←or→ to make yourself happy?

2555. Float into the air holding a bunch of balloons ←or→ ride atop a racing train?

2556. Do nothing at all ←or→ do something?

2557. Pants ←or→ kilts?

2558. Interact with clowns ←or→ with mimes?

2559. Play with a wolf ←or→ play with a hyena?

2560. Drink from a water bottle ←or→ a water spigot?

2561. Eat garlic flavored ←or→ anchovy flavored ice cream?

2562. Tennis ←or→ backgammon?

2563. Rugby ←or→ American football?

2564. Have long flowing locks ←or→ short sassy curls?

2565. Be the one leaving ←or→ be the one left behind?

2566. See brake lights ←or→ headlights?

2567. Accept your fate ←or→ make your fate happen?

2568. Drive a convertible top down in the rain ←or→ in the snow?

2569. Swallow a pill ←or→ drink bitter medicine?

2570. Choose to do nothing ←or→ choose to do something?

2571. Be a worker bee ←or→ the queen bee?

2572. Go down a rabbit hole ←or→ into a bear cave?

2573. Endure a shipwreck ←or→ be lost in space?

2574. Run with wolves ←or→ swim with sharks?

2575. Be in shark-infested seas ←or→ piranha infested rivers?

2576. Wear sunglasses at night ←or→ wear a swimsuit in the winter?

2577. Glasses ←or→ laser vision correction?

2578. See it rain cats and dogs ←or→ pigs fly?

2579. Wander the Australian outback ←or→ the African Sahara?

2580. Suck a tart lemon ←or→ eat three tablespoons of salt?

2581. Explore an abandoned haunted building ←or→ an abandoned haunted ship?

2582. Be haunted ←or→ be the one haunting?

2583. Be a blood sucking vampire ←or→ an energy sucking vampire?

2584. Have it be spring for two years straight ←or→ fall?

2585. Build sandcastles ←or→ make mud pies?

2586. Live next to a bunch of rowdy teenagers ←or→ a group of senior citizens?

2587. Crab ←or→ lobster?

2588. Write with a pen ←or→ pencil?

2589. Peanut butter and jelly ←or→ peanut butter, honey, and bananas?

2590. Float in the clouds ←or→ dance on a rainbow?

2591. Follow a trail of ants ←or→ a group of roaches?

2592. Dress 50 mannequins ←or→ 50 chihuahuas?

2593. Be a member of a boy band ←or→ a girl group?

2594. Read and write everything in morse code ←or→ hieroglyphics?

2595. Play tennis ←or→ go bowling?

2596. Soar like an eagle ←or→ float like a duck?

2597. Wrestle with a crocodile ←or→ with a great white shark?

2598. Give a donation ←or→ receive a donation?

2599. Stir up a hornet's nest ←or→ a wasp's?

2600. Go to the zoo ←or→ to an amusement park?

2601. Read Chaucer ←or→ Shakespeare?

2602. Mushrooms on your pizza ←or→ olives?

2603. Have scars ←or→ tattoos?

2604. Make a wish in a well ←or→ in a water fountain?

2605. Only be able to moan when someone asks you a question ←or→ groan when they ask?

2606. French fries ←or→ potato wedges?

2607. Chase a squirrel ←or→ a chipmunk?

2608. Roll around in poison ivy ←or→ give up your salary for three months?

2609. Pearls ←or→ diamonds?

2610. Encounter a bull ←or→ a moose?

2611. Confess to a crime you didn't commit and earn 50 million dollars ←or→ admit you didn't do it and get nothing?

2612. Split cab fare to get to your destination faster ←or→ ride solo and take the longer way?

2613. Be the antidote to every virus, known or not, and save the world, living in a lab all your life ←or→ keep it quiet and let the world suffer?

2614. Eat a raw potato ←or→ a raw onion?

2615. Be successful at everything you do and have no friends ←or→ be a major screw up and have many friends?

2616. Have an apple ←or→ a chocolate chip cookie?

2617. Go into politics ←or→ join a secret society?

2618. Have a missing front tooth ←or→
let your dad go out partying with your friends?

2619. Paint a house ←or→ paint a bus?

2620. Be a security guard at a hospital ←or→ a mall cop?

2621. Be the buyer ←or→ the seller?

2622. Be stuck in a dungeon ←or→ in an outdoor toilet?

2623. Just walk away from an argument ←or→ stay and fight?

2624. Travel to Europe ←or→ Asia?

2625. Soup ←or→ chowder?

2626. Be artistic ←or→ analytical?

2627. Come across a tortoise ←or→ a sea turtle?

2628. Work as a dentist ←or→ as a podiatrist?

2629. Be indoors at all times ←or→ outdoors at all times?

2630. Be extremely organized ←or→ an absolute hot mess?

2631. Speak in nothing but slogans ←or→ speak in only the phonetic alphabet?

2632. Whipped frosting ←or→ buttercream frosting?

2633. Spend all your money for one perfectly wonderful day and be poor the rest of your life ←or→ be wealthy with nothing but bad days?

2634. Work in London ←or→ New York?

2635. Run a country ←or→ a business?

2636. Be famous in your career ←or→ celebrity famous?

2637. Write a best-selling book ←or→ win an Olympic gold medal?

2638. Live in France ←or→ Italy?

2639. Give up your music ←or→ TV streaming channel?

2640. Wake up early ←or→ go to bed late?

2641. Wear professional attire ←or→ business casual on Friday?

2642. Live in Lagos ←or→ Abu Dhabi?

2643. Watch TV shows ←or→ movies?

2644. Read physical books ←or→ ebooks?

2645. Have a nice car ←or→ nice home?

2646. Find personal bad news out on social media ←or→ receive a phone call?

2647. Step on a toy barefoot ←or→ get a paper cut?

2648. Have no eyebrows ←or→ no fingernails?

2649. Eat a cat ←or→ a dog?

2650. Have diarrhea ←or→ the flu?

2651. Go streaking ←or→ go cliff diving?

2652. Pay twice as much for a plane ticket ←or→ never be able to fly?

2653. Go blind young but always have a full head of hair ←or→
go bald young but never lose your sight?

2654. Have night sweats ←or→ night terrors?

2655. Drink only one cup of coffee for the rest of your life ←or→
never be able to drink coffee again?

2656. Have your thumbs replaced with big toes ←or→
your pinkies replaced with pinky toes?

2657. Climb a small mountain to get to work every day ←or→
swim across 100-foot river to get to work every day?

2658. Have lots of energy ←or→ lots of money?

2659. Have really slow internet ←or→ always have really bad phone signal?

2660. Lick your best friend's foot ←or→ let a stranger lick your foot?

2661. Be able to change one thing in your past ←or→
have a get out of jail free card?

2662. Spend every weekend indoors ←or→ spend every weekend outdoors?

2663. Wear high heels to bed ←or→ wear bedroom slippers anywhere you go?

2664. Never be able to do a good smoky eye ←or→
never be able to do perfect lips?

2665. Buy 10 things you don't need every time you went to the store ←or→
always forget one thing you needed when you go to the store?

2666. Cut your nails too short every time ←or→ burn your tongue on hot drinks?

2667. Be the strongest person in the world ←or→
the fastest person in the world?

2668. Go to a museum ←or→ go to a library?

2669. Wander around aimlessly ←or→ walk with purpose?

2670. Help a child with complicated homework ←or→ cook dinner?

2671. Would you rather eat a toasted marshmallow ←or→ a plain one?

2672. Walk a long distance in a parking lot to save dings on your car ←or→
park closer and chance the dings?

2673. Fly a kite ←or→ ride a bicycle?

2674. Trust a stranger ←or→ choose to go with your untrustworthy friend?

2675. Choose a red button ←or→ a blue one?

2676. Have your birthday party outside ←or→ indoors?

2677. Have skeletons in your closet ←or→ be an open book?

2678. Help a stranger in need ←or→ a toxic friend you've known forever?

2679. Wear a different onesie every day for a year ←or→
a furry tuxedo during the hottest week of the year?

2680. Rocks, paper ←or→ scissors?

2681. Be honest about all of your faults ←or→ be blissfully unaware?

2682. Pick trash off the side of highways for community service ←or→
work in a soup kitchen?

2683. Use a calculator to add and subtract ←or→
use your fingers and your toes?

2684. Walk with a stuffed teddy bear everywhere you go ←or→ with a doll?

2685. Eat a whole tomato ←or→ eat a kumquat?

2686. Picnic in a park ←or→ sunbathe on the beach?

2687. Take a stairway to heaven ←or→ take the highway to hell?

2688. Change your bath towels every month ←or→
every week if you're the only one who will do the laundry?

2689. Live by a daily goal ←or→ a monthly goal?

2690. Eat a green apple with a worm in it ←or→ not eat at all and starve?

2691. Have the ability to separate from your body and go into that of other people and live their lives ←or→ always be you?

2692. Wish upon a twinkling star ←or→ wish on a shooting comet?

2693. Move forward trusting the bad ending would be followed by a new beginning ←or→ stay perfectly still?

2694. Wear a suit of armor every day of winter ←or→ a snow suit every day of summer?

2695. Give an interview ←or→ be interviewed?

2696. Do a headstand for an hour ←or→ do continual cartwheels for an hour?

2697. Own your mistakes ←or→ be unapologetic?

2698. Use an automated navigation system ←or→ a hard copy road map?

2699. Eat sugar cookies ←or→ chocolate chip cookies?

2700. Write research papers every day for three years ←or→ write blog posts every day for a website for twenty years?

2701. Cut the grass of a huge lawn ←or→ chopped down thick foliage and intertwined vines growing all over the house?

2702. Live in Asia ←or→ Africa?

2703. Go by a childhood nickname that embarrassed you ←or→ have everyone always mispronounce your name?

2704. Ice cream ←or→ pudding?

2705. Have a pet whale ←or→ a pet walrus?

2706. Not be able to hear others ←or→ not be able to hear yourself?

2707. Live in your favorite video game ←or→ live in your favorite movie?

2708. Save your mother ←or→ your significant other from a psychopathic killer?

2709. Cough all the time ←or→ feel the urge to pee all the time?

2710. Hear everything on a three second delay ←or→
three seconds earlier then everyone else?

2711. Be stuck on a deserted island with a selfish person ←or→ a lazy person?

2712. Be stuck on an island with a lazy person ←or→ a rude person?

2713. Be stuck on an island with a selfish person ←or→ a rude person?

2714. Have triangle cut sandwiches ←or→ sandwiches cut in halves?

2715. Wear clean clothes when you're dirty ←or→
wear dirty clothes when you're clean?

2716. Die fast ←or→ survive long enough to live in a post-apocalyptic world?

2717. Read a book that's great but has a bad ending ←or→
a book that's horrible but has a great ending?

2718. Be hospitalized due to an illness ←or→ an injury?

2719. Be a con artist ←or→ a serial killer?

2720. Have a magical wand ←or→ a magical staff?

2721. Wear make-up ←or→ go natural?

2722. Have the power to gain everyone's trust ←or→
be invulnerable to any harm?

2723. Have a self-driving automobile ←or→ drive it yourself?

2724. Choose all truths ←or→ all dares?

2725. Speak only truths ←or→ tell only lies?

2726. Be well rested but miss your plans ←or→
be tired but attend your all your plans?

2727. Never use toilet paper again ←or→ never use hair products again?

2728. Cry every night before falling asleep ←or→
cry every morning when you wake?

2729. Live on Mars ←or→ Venus?

2730. Be the best at being the worst ←or→ the worst at being the best?

2731. Get good sleep ←or→ have delicious food?

2732. Have a stuffy nose ←or→ a runny nose?

2733. Be the best spy in the world that no one has ever heard of ←or→ the most well-known criminal on the run?

2734. Have free food ←or→ free rent for life?

2735. Float for eternity in space ←or→ under water?

2736. Learn everything 10x faster ←or→ instantly master 10 things of your choosing?

2737. Be the only happy person in a world of unhappy people ←or→ the only unhappy person in a world of happy people?

2738. Live in a world with human sized mosquitos ←or→ dog sized spiders?

2739. Know the winning numbers to the next lottery ←or→ know exactly how the stock market is going to go?

2740. Use ceiling fans ←or→ floor fans?

2741. Have debilitating loneliness ←or→ a toxic marriage?

2742. Have severe financial difficulty ←or→ chronic health issues?

2743. Be mortal ←or→ a god?

2744. Life in a fairytale world of magic of your choice ←or→ a sci-fi world of your choice?

2745. Be trapped in an elevator for three days ←or→ trapped underground in a mine?

2746. Never have to shower again ←or→
never have to go to the bathroom again?

2747. Be extremely selfless ←or→ extremely selfish?

2748. Have an incredible amount of luck ←or→
have an incredible amount of skill?

2749. Be a main character in a horror film ←or→
a side character in a small town mystery?

2750. See one of your exes' face every time you look in the mirror ←or→
never be in another relationship again?

2751. Live with elves ←or→ dwarves?

2752. Give up bread ←or→ cheese?

2753. Be able to stop time for as long as you can hold your breath ←or→
fast forward time every time you to sneeze?

2754. Live in a black and white world ←or→ a world only in pastel colors?

2755. Have a solar powered water pump ←or→ a solar power fridge?

2756. Meet a time traveler from the future ←or→ an alien from another planet?

2757. Meet your guardian angel ←or→ the Grim Reaper?

2758. Live in a world where it's always raining ←or→ always snowing?

2759. Live in a world without dogs ←or→ a world without cats?

2760. Be in physical pain ←or→ emotional pain?

2761. Gender swap with someone else ←or→ be who you are?

2762. Receive half everything in the universe ←or→ get double of some things?

2763. Be immune to dying of old age ←or→
be immune to being killed by external forces?

2764. Have the sun disappear for two months ←or→
have aliens arrive on Earth today?

2765. Be able to taste with your hands ←or→ taste with your feet?

2766. Be an eagle for a week ←or→ a leopard for a day?

2767. Eat noodles with too much water ←or→ too little?

2768. Rather have loved and lost ←or→ never have loved at all?

2769. Learn the meaning of love ←or→ the meaning of life?

2770. Be able to fly ←or→ teleport?

2771. Be on a broken ski lift ←or→ in a broken elevator?

2772. Be able to talk to dogs ←or→ be able to turn into a dog
whenever you want?

2773. Have very loud neighbors ←or→ very nosy neighbors?

2774. Hit the gym ←or→ hit the couch?

2775. Win free airfare for life ←or→ free hotel stays for life?

2776. Remodel your bathroom ←or→
remodel your bedroom if you won a load of cash?

2777. Look five years older ←or→ five years younger?

2778. Grow horns ←or→ grow a tail?

2779. Keep the left side ←or→ the right side if you were cut in half vertically?

2780. Have someone hate you ←or→ feel indifferent towards you?

2781. Cucumbers ←or→ zucchinis?

2782. Be a mythical creature ←or→ a sci-fi creature?

2783. Have all your clothes be two sizes too small ←or→
have to say everything twice?

2784. Date for love ←or→ date for money?

2785. Permanently have the feeling you're about to sneeze ←or→
the feeling of having pins and needles in your feet?

2786. Have a permanent big smile on your face ←or→
never be able to look anyone in the eye?

2787. Stub your toe ←or→ get a splinter in your finger?

2788. Be too quick at everything ←or→ too slow at everything?

2789. Send a letter to a friend ←or→ receive a letter from a friend?

2790. Be annoyed by everyone you meet ←or→ never be taken seriously?

2791. Be buried ←or→ cremated?

2792. Be an eagle ←or→ a jellyfish?

2793. Be twice as slow ←or→ half your height?

2794. Have a pet dog ←or→ pet dragon?

2795. Let your talent go to waste and do nothing ←or→
use your talent but be forced to always perform challenging tasks?

2796. Have a small house and expensive car ←or→
an expensive house and a rundown car?

2797. Live a life only saying yes ←or→ a life only saying no?

2798. Be a teen forever ←or→ be elderly forever?

2799. Compose the best music album of all time ←or→
create the best videogame of all time?

2800. Have a water balloon fight ←or→ a snowball fight?

2801. Have the same drink flavor for the rest of your life ←or→
have a new drink flavor every day with no repeats?

2802. Consume a whole gallon of mustard ←or→ of ketchup?

2803. Fight a crocodile ←or→ an anaconda?

2804. Be able to understand trees and flowers ←or→ speak to animals?

2805. Live in a lighthouse ←or→ in a clock tower?

2806. Be considered bloodthirsty ←or→ wise?

2807. Live in the west ←or→ the east?

2808. Revolt ←or→ champion peace?

2809. Be hungry ←or→ eat night crawlers?

2810. Be considered bewitching ←or→ frustrating?

2811. Plant seeds ←or→ eat them?

2812. Follow guidelines ←or→ make your own rules?

2813. Live as an animal ←or→ as a tree?

2814. Live in paradise but be unhappy ←or→ live in a hovel but be happy?

2815. Listen to music from headphones ←or→ loudly from the speakers?

2816. Fight against injustice and be arrested ←or→ keep quiet and remain free?

2817. Be a hawk ←or→ a dove?

2818. Be an observer ←or→ someone considered abrasive?

2819. Receive presents from others ←or→ give presents to others?

2820. Be carnivorous ←or→ a vegetarian?

2821. Encounter a ghoulish apparition ←or→ a bloodthirsty weretiger?

2822. Heavy sweaters ←or→ heavy coats?

2823. Have a friend that always tells you the truth ←or→
a friend who always backs you up even when you're wrong?

2824. Have a little rock in your shoe you can't find ←or→
a hangnail that catches on everything?

2825. Work hard to earn a dollar ←or→ inherit a million?

2826. Have lips made of teeth ←or→ teeth made of lips?

2827. Receive a guaranteed $500 ←or→
take a chance on getting a larger amount?

2828. Find a dream partner ←or→ a dream job?

2829. Be able to have mind control on other people ←or→
put words into other people's mouths?

2830. Have severely chapped lips ←or→ a bloody nose?

2831. Have a free day off every Friday ←or→ every Monday?

2832. Die before your significant other ←or→ after your significant other?

2833. Have long hair growing out of your nose ←or→ long hair growing out of
your ears?

2834. Have to tell everyone you meet that you love them ←or→ never be able to say you love anyone?

2835. Have unlimited wealth ←or→ unlimited knowledge?

2836. Kiss a poisonous toad ←or→ a poisonous spider?

2837. Give up pizza forever ←or→ give up coffee forever?

2838. Only be able to tell food is rotten by tasting it ←or→ have all the food you eat smell rotten even though its fine?

2839. Be able to take a shower whenever you want but have low water pressure ←or→ take a perfect shower only once a month?

2840. Wear no socks ←or→ no underwear for an entire year?

2841. Have unlimited pencils with no erasers ←or→ unlimited pens in only one color?

2842. Have a bad hair day ←or→ a bad clothes day?

2843. Live in a world ruled by robots ←or→ a world ruled by aliens?

2844. Travel by hippo ←or→ by kangaroo?

2845. Watch a movie behind an extremely tall person ←or→ with a friend who talks the entire time?

2846. Have a bad haircut ←or→ shave your head bald?

2847. Look and feel 10 years younger from the neck up ←or→
from the neck down?

2848. Live next to a graveyard ←or→ in a haunted house?

2849. Spend five years in prison ←or→ 20 years in a coma?

2850. Marry your perfect partner ←or→ achieve all of your dreams and be alone?

2851. Be well fed and homeless ←or→ have a home and little food for a month?

2852. Have a car that always has fuel ←or→
a car that never needs to be repaired?

2853. Be in a room with only one movie to watch ←or→ one book to read?

2854. Invent something for the first time ←or→
discover something for the first time?

2855. Eat ants in your ice cream ←or→ worms in your soup?

2856. Have no feelings ←or→ be overly emotional?

2857. Have no one attend your funeral ←or→ no one attend your wedding?

2858. Have a personal chef ←or→ a personal driver?

2859. Always wear wet gloves ←or→ wet shoes?

2860. Earn a dollar for each word you say ←or→ each step you take?

2861. Live in an RV ←or→ live on a sailboat?

2862. Your parents ←or→ your boss have access to everything on your phone?

2863. Get nothing on your birthday ←or→ get 100 gifts you absolutely hated?

2864. Date someone who talks too much during movies ←or→ wears too much cologne/perfume?

2865. Have a friend that types in all caps ←or→ a friend that replies to all in email?

2866. Burn your tongue ←or→ burn the top of your mouth?

2867. Have a terrible tattoo that's always visible ←or→ a horrible scar that's only partially visible?

2868. Watch TV that is commercial-free, but you don't have a remote control ←or→ have a remote control but have to watch all the commercials?

2869. Eat all your meals with someone who chews loudly ←or→ with someone who chews with their mouth open?

2870. Know a little about a lot of topics ←or→ a lot about a few topics?

2871. Know what everyone is thinking ←or→ see into everyone's future?

2872. Never eat your favorite food again ←or→ never kiss someone again?

2873. Spend the rest of your life without music ←or→ without movies?

2874. Lose all the toes on one foot ←or→ lose one of your ears?

2875. Go a year without combing your hair ←or→ a year without deodorant?

2876. Have unlimited strength ←or→ unlimited speed?

2877. Have every outfit you wear fit too small ←or→ be too itchy?

2878. Never get angry ←or→ never get jealous?

2879. Receive a $300 discount on everything you buy ←or→
receive a 40% discount on everything you buy?

2880. Eat nothing but burnt food ←or→
nothing but leftovers from people you don't know?

2881. Receive cake as a gift from someone ←or→ candy?

2882. Live in luxury in a town you hate ←or→ a shack in a town you love?

2883. Have no long-term memory ←or→ no short-term memory?

2884. Not have knees ←or→ not have elbows?

2885. Have a job where you can sit all day ←or→ you stand all day?

2886. Live in a nest ←or→ live in a den?

2887. Have there only be one of you ←or→ have a clone?

2888. Play mobile games ←or→ console games?

2889. Listen to music ←or→ podcasts while walking?

2890. Cardio ←or→ weights for exercise?

2891. Toast ←or→ eggs?

2892. Be a rich friend ←or→ a loyal friend?

2893. Work hard ←or→ play hard?

2894. Do dirty laundry ←or→ wash dirty dishes?

2895. Wear sneakers ←or→ sandals?

2896. Sit on a couch ←or→ in a recliner?

2897. Be the passenger ←or→ the driver?

2898. Work on a tablet ←or→ a computer?

2899. Receive a postal letter ←or→ an email?

2900. Have loads of money ←or→ loads of free time?

2901. Spend a day at an amusement park ←or→ a day at the beach?

2902. Have popcorn ←or→ candy at the movies?

2903. Pancakes ←or→ waffles?

2904. Blinds ←or→ curtains?

2905. Save your money ←or→ spend your money?

2906. Soup ←or→ sandwich?

2907. Battle ninjas ←or→ pirates?

2908. Deep sea diving ←or→ bungee jumping?

2909. Have x-ray vision ←or→ bionic hearing?

2910. Go on a cruise with friends ←or→ with your spouse?

2911. Meet your ancestors ←or→ your great-great-great grandchildren?

2912. Lead a boring life from here forward ←or→
be reborn into a baby of another gender?

2913. Have your tears be acidic ←or→ sweat maple syrup?

2914. Have a closet of nothing but plaid flannel ←or→
a closet of nothing but denim?

2915. Have your home be underwater ←or→ your home be in the side of a cliff?

2916. Have stretchable legs ←or→ have stretchable arms?

2917. Have teatime ←or→ a coffee break?

2918. Marry a new, random person every year ←or→
marry one, random person and stick it out with them?

2919. Have a month of nonstop intense tropical storm-like rain ←or→
a month of 100+ degree heatwaves?

2920. Not know how to read ←or→ not know how to write?

2921. Stand on a bed of burning hot coals for at least 30 seconds ←or→ stick your hand in a waffle iron maker for two minutes?

2922. Always disappoint people ←or→ always anger them?

2923. Use a jet pack ←or→ a hovercraft?

2924. Star in a cartoon movie ←or→ star in a live action movie?

2925. Watch only dramas for the rest of your life ←or→ watch only comedies for the rest of your life?

2926. Always announce every historical date in the world ←or→ know everyone's birthday and/or anniversary?

2927. Never be able to compliment another person ←or→ never be able to complain?

2928. Be on jury duty ←or→ go to work?

2929. Get $20K worth of jewelry ←or→ $10K worth of electronics?

2930. Be covered in fur ←or→ covered in feathers?

2931. Speak in nothing but swear words ←or→ never be able to swear again?

2932. Write a book ←or→ paint a picture?

2933. Control the elements ←or→ control time?

2934. Have the ability to have full control over your dreams ←or→ never have to sleep?

2935. Be credited with the invention of the wheel ←or→
be credited with the invention of the Internet?

2936. Be a righty ←or→ a lefty?

2937. Sing everything you say ←or→ do interpretive dancing
for everything you want to communicate?

2938. Eat a meal of only jellybeans ←or→ a meal of only hot wings?

2939. Drink only milk ←or→ orange juice for the rest of your life?

2940. Die in a zombie apocalypse ←or→ die in a nuclear war?

2941. Let bygones be bygones ←or→ exact your revenge?

2942. Keep trying to use a remote that's not working ←or→
just go change the batteries?

2943. Attend a film festival ←or→ a music festival?

2944. Spend your time in your front yard ←or→ in your back yard?

2945. Be more like your mom ←or→ your dad?

2946. Be responsible for putting a man on the moon ←or→
inventing wheels on luggage?

2947. Take a risk ←or→ play it safe?

2948. Be responsible for the accidental death of a child ←or→
of three adults?

2949. Be a fencer ←or→ a jouster?

2950. Be known as the person who gives the best gifts ←or→ the person who makes the best cakes?

2951. Have many little regrets in your life ←or→ just one major regret in your life?

2952. Be locked in a room that is constantly dark for a week ←or→ a room that is constantly bright for a week?

2953. Have low fat foods ←or→ no fat foods?

2954. Wear shoes with laces ←or→ slip-ons?

2955. Be a twin ←or→ a triplet?

2956. Have a lava lamp in your room ←or→ a strobe light?

2957. Eat poison ivy ←or→ a handful of bumblebees?

2958. Deliver quiet good news ←or→ exciting bad news?

2959. Celebrate your birthday every day of the year ←or→ a job promotion one time?

2960. Be able to change your mind ←or→ make a decision and stick to it?

2961. Always get the joke ←or→ never get the joke?

2962. Be able to find everything for everyone that is lost ←or→ find the most valuable thing for one person one time?

2963. Solve the world's environmental pollution ←or→
solve the world's health crisis?

2964. Be able to fix a broken sink ←or→ fix a broken stove?

2965. Share your problems with family and ease your own stress ←or→
keep your problems to yourself and spare putting your stress on family?

2966. Ride a motorcycle ←or→ a jet ski?

2967. Go on a limitless shopping spree for one day ←or→
have free buffet for the rest of your life?

2968. French fries ←or→ onion rings?

2969. Stay in the country you're in for the rest of your life ←or→
move to another to live forever?

2970. Do everything without question ←or→
question everything and never get anything done?

2971. Raw oysters ←or→ raw mussels?

2972. Eat from a bent spoon ←or→ a bent fork?

2973. Be involved in a major political scandal ←or→
a social networking scandal?

2974. Watch what you say because you have a lot riding on it ←or→
speak your truth and risk everything?

2975. Medical treatment ←or→ holistic treatment for ailments?

2976. Apologize to make peace (even if you're right) ←or→ stand by your beliefs?

2977. Be the one who always follows advice ←or→
the one who always gives advice?

2978. Live the rest of your life taking a plane from one place to another ←or→
driving an RV from one place to another?

2979. Catch fish to feed others ←or→
teach others to fish so they can feed themselves?

2980. Drink a gallon of slime ←or→ swallow a dozen raw eggs?

2981. Be the goalkeeper ←or→ playing the field?

2982. Be the one to lend everything ←or→ the one who borrows everything?

2983. Tolerate the bad behavior of everyone around you ←or→
tell them about themselves and start conflict?

2984. Have a chimpanzee ←or→ a panda for a pet?

2985. Read about history ←or→ be the one making history?

2986. Own a fleet of trucks ←or→ own a fleet of ships?

2987. Be able to hear only the positive things people say about you ←or→
only the negative things people say about you?

2988. Let a random person cut your hair ←or→ let a random person
color your hair?

2989. Be a multi-millionaire living in the 1900 ←or→ a middle-class person living today?

2990. Be able to talk to wild animals ←or→ domesticated animals?

2991. Have a perfect significant other but no friends ←or→ friends but an imperfect significant other?

2992. Eat delicious food with a blind date every night for an entire month ←or→ eat fast food with a good friend every night for an entire month?

2993. Date your best friend's sibling ←or→ have your best friend date your sibling?

2994. Eat the best meal with no utensils ←or→ a mediocre meal with utensils?

2995. Work a high-paying job that you absolutely hate ←or→ a low-paying job you absolutely love?

2996. Be in a talent show ←or→ a school play?

2997. Be the lead in a musical ←or→ blend in with the chorus?

2998. Dance at your mom's wedding ←or→ have your mom dance at your wedding?

2999. Dream about your crush but never meet them ←or→ meet your crush but they forget you as soon as you walk away?

3000. Oatmeal with raisins ←or→ oatmeal with brown sugar?

3001. Be able to forge signatures ←or→ forge checks?